BrightRED Study Guide

CfE ADVANCED Higher

HISTORY

Ross MacLachlan

First published in 2022 by:
Bright Red Publishing Ltd

Copyright © Bright Red Publishing Ltd 2022 Cover image © Caleb Rutherford

All rights reserved. No part of this publication may be reproduced, stored in a retrieval system, or transmitted in any form or by any means, electronic, mechanical, photocopying, recording or otherwise, without prior permission in writing from the publisher.

The rights of Ross MacLachlan to be identified as the author of this work have been asserted by him in accordance with Sections 77 and 78 of the Copyright, Designs and Patents Act 1988.

A CIP record for this book is available from the British Library.

ISBN 978-1-84948-310-0

With thanks to:
PDQ Digital Media Solutions Ltd, Bungay (layout) and Ivor Normound (copy-edit).
Cover design and series book design by Caleb Rutherford – e i d e t i c.

Acknowledgements

Every effort has been made to seek all copyright-holders. If any have been overlooked, then Bright Red Publishing will be delighted to make the necessary arrangements.

Permission has been sought from all relevant copyright holders and Bright Red Publishing are grateful for the use of the following:

fizkes/Shutterstock.com (p 5); LBeddoe/Shutterstock.com (p 6); Princess_Anmitsu/Shutterstock.com (p 7); Kubko/Shutterstock.com (p 8 top); Andrey_Popov/Shutterstock.com (p 8 bottom); Eiko Tsuchiya/Shutterstock.com (p 9 top); BKHRB/Shutterstock.com (p 9 middle); ADragan/Shutterstock.com (p 9 bottom); StunningArt/Shutterstock.com (p 10); Lois GoBe/Shutterstock.com (p 12 top); Ray49/Shutterstock.com (p 12 bottom); NuPenDekDee/Shutterstock.com (p 16); mohdizuan/Shutterstock.com (p 18 top); vlastas/Shutterstock.com (p 18 bottom); Everett Collection/Shutterstock.com (p 19); Alexander_Kuzmin/Shutterstock.com (p 21); Dima Aslanian/Shutterstock.com (p 23); Monster Ztudio/Shutterstock.com (p 24); Triff/Shutterstock.com (p 25); juras10/Shutterstock.com (p 26 top); Zakharova_Elena/Shutterstock.com (p 26 bottom); extract from *Heinemann Advanced History: Germany 1919-45* by Martin Collier & Philip Pedley, © 2000. Reprinted by permission of Pearson Education Limited (p 36); extract from *The Romans who shaped Britiain* by Sam Moorhead and David Stuttard. Copyright © 2012 Thames & Hudson Ltd, London (p 40); Arthur Bargan/Shutterstock.com (p 42); stoatphoto/Shutterstock.com (p 44); Song_about_summer/Shutterstock.com (p 46); ESB Professional/Shutterstock.com (p 47); OlgaPS/Shutterstock.com (p 48); grufnar/Shutterstock.com (p 50); Mar Fernandez/Shutterstock.com (p 52); Microsoft OneNote screenshot used with permission from Microsoft (p 53); Abert/Shutterstock.com (p 55); stoatphoto/Shutterstock.com (p 56); Microsoft Word screenshot used with permission from Microsoft (p 57); d_odin/Shutterstock.com (p 59); Camera Nation/Shutterstock.com (p 64); Vuk Kostic/Shutterstock.com (p 65); PJ_Photography/Shutterstock.com (p 66); affordable_cat/Shutterstock.com (p 67); Fulcanelli/Shutterstock.com (p 68); Bill McKelvie/Shutterstock.com (p 69); vlastas/Shutterstock.com (p 70); Scottish Andrew/Shutterstock.com (p 72); Jan Holm/Shutterstock.com (p 75); Everett Collection/Shutterstock.com (p 78); Jim Pruitt/Shutterstock.com (p 79); Enrique Ramos/Shutterstock.com (p 80); Mihai_Andritoiu/Shutterstock.com (p 81 top left); Everett Collection/Shutterstock.com (pp 81 top right & 82); Kevin Esterline/Shutterstock.com (p 83); Everett Collection/Shutterstock.com (pp 86, 87, 88, 90, 91); Ksanti/Shutterstock.com (p 92); SALNIKOV MIKHAIL/Shutterstock.com (p 95).

Printed and bound in the UK.

CONTENTS

INTRODUCTION TO ADVANCED HIGHER HISTORY
The Advanced Higher History Course 4

PREPARING FOR THE QUESTION PAPER
Organisation 6
Condensing Your Notes 8
Review and Information Retrieval 10
In the Exam 12

THE QUESTION PAPER, PART 1 – ESSAY QUESTIONS
The Nature of the Essay Questions 14
Marking Criteria and Structuring Your Essay 16
Structure Criteria – Introductions 18
Constructing the Main Body of Your Essay 20
Historical Sources and Interpretations Criteria 22
Structure Criteria –
Mini-Conclusions and Conclusions 24

THE QUESTION PAPER, PART 2 – SOURCE-HANDLING QUESTIONS
Question Types and an Explanation
of Components of Source-Handling Questions 26
The "Evaluate the Usefulness …" Question 28
Writing Your Answer to the "Evaluate the
Usefulness …" Question 30
Alternative Structures for the "Evaluate the
Usefulness …" Question 32
The "How Fully …?" Question and how to answer it .. 34
Alternative Structures for the "How Fully …?"
Question 36
The "Interpretation of Two Sources" Question
and how to answer it 38
Alternative Structures for the "Interpretation of
Two Sources" Question 40

THE DISSERTATION
Introduction to the Dissertation 42
Planning Your Dissertation 44
Selecting Texts and Resources 46
Deadlines and Record-keeping 48
Carrying out Reading 50
Taking Effective Notes – Part 1 52
Taking Effective Notes – Part 2 54
Referencing – Part 1 56
Referencing – Part 2 58
The Structure and Presentation of Your Dissertation . 60
The Layout of the Title Page, Contents Page
and Bibliography 62

SUMMARIES OF REVISION NOTES
Northern Britain from the Iron Age to AD 1034 64
Scotland: Independence and Kingship, 1249–1334 ... 72
USA: "A House Divided": 1850–1865 78
Germany: From Democracy to Dictatorship,
1918–1939 84
Russia: From Tsarism to Stalinism, 1914–1945 90

INTRODUCTION TO ADVANCED HIGHER HISTORY

THE ADVANCED HIGHER HISTORY COURSE

STRUCTURE OF THE COURSE

There are two units in the Advanced Higher History course which you will complete.

Advanced Higher History

Historical Study
For this part of the course, you will study one period in history, considering a variety of historical issues and controversies through the use of a wide range of sources. This will be tested in the written exam. There are ten fields of study that can be chosen from. Unlike Higher History, where three topics are learned, only one will be selected for the Advanced Higher course. The options are as follows:
1. Northern Britain from the Iron Age to AD 1034
2. Scotland: Independence and Kingship, 1249–1334
3. Scotland: From the Treaty of Union to the Enlightenment, 1707–1815
4. USA: "A House Divided", 1850–1865
5. Japan: The Modernisation of a Nation, 1840–1920
6. Germany: From Democracy to Dictatorship, 1918–1939
7. South Africa: Race and Power, 1902–1984
8. Russia: From Tsarism to Stalinism, 1914–1945
9. Spain: The Civil War – Causes, Conflict and Consequences, 1923–1945
10. Britain: At War and Peace, 1938–1951

Historical Research
For this part of the course, you will plan, research and present on a historical issue of your choice, within your field of study. This will be examined through submission of a dissertation.

ONLINE

The SQA Advanced Higher History website lists the content included in each of the Fields of Study. Open the "Course and Unit Support Notes" and scroll down to the table that relates to your specific field of study. The Key Issues give you the topic headings that you will study, and these are detailed further in the Description of Content. Find the link at www.brightredbooks.net/subjects

DON'T FORGET

The source-handling questions will only examine the *italicised* illustrative examples within your fields of study. Check the SQA Course and Unit Support Notes for this.

OPTIONAL UNIT ASSESSMENT

There are two unit assessments that can be sat independently. The first focuses on extended response and source-handling skills. The second will examine the research and writing process of your dissertation. Passing Unit Assessments is no longer a requirement to gain a Course Award (Grade A–D). They can now be achieved instead of obtaining a full course award.

HOW THE COURSE IS GRADED

The grade you receive will be determined solely by your performance in the written exam and the dissertation. Combined, these two components are worth 140 marks. If successful, you will be awarded Grade A, B, C or D.

The written exam

The duration of the written exam is three hours, and it is worth 90 marks. All marks are distributed to questions specifically linked to your chosen field of study. The exam has two parts:

contd

Introduction to Advanced Higher History: The Advanced Higher History Course

1. Part 1 (Historical Issues) is worth 50 marks. You will complete two essays, worth 25 marks each. There will be five essay questions for you to choose from in your field of study.

2. Part 2 (Historical Sources) is worth 40 marks. There will be four sources specific to your field of study for you to consider, which could be written or pictorial. You will complete three source-handling questions: one "Evaluate the usefulness ..." question, worth 12 marks; one "How fully ...?" question, worth 12 marks; and one "Interpretation of Two Sources" question, worth 16 marks.

It is important to realise that while Part 1 could examine any section of the Key Issues or Description of Content in your field of study, Part 2 is more selective. In the Scottish Qualifications Authority (SQA) Course and Unit Support Notes, you will find that there are *italicised* and non-italicised parts of the Description of Content. Only the *italicised* content will be examined in Part 2, i.e. the source-handling questions.

The dissertation

Sometimes referred to as the Added Value Unit or AVU, or the Assignment, the dissertation is worth 50 marks. The title of your dissertation will be chosen by you, from a set list of titles within your field of study produced by the SQA. It can be seen as a larger version of the essays you will be writing in preparation for the final exam, and has a limit of 4,000 words.

The dissertation will allow you to research more deeply into an issue within your field of study and formally present your findings. It is a piece of coursework which you plan, research and write independently of work completed for the exam. You are expected to read widely from a number of authors and sources and to present your findings in a coherent manner. The final version of your dissertation will be sent to the SQA to be graded.

 THINGS TO DO AND THINK ABOUT

To be successful in this course, you need to be organised and motivated. It is essential that you regularly condense your class and reading notes into more manageable revision summaries. You also need to read over these regularly in order to effectively memorise key information. Finally, it is important that you spread the reading and writing of your dissertation throughout the year to provide yourself with time to rectify any problems that may arise in your research.

PREPARING FOR THE QUESTION PAPER

ORGANISATION

The final exam is a challenge that is best met by preparing early. You need to be highly organised in order to process and revise the volume of information required to be able to write for three hours. The topics in this chapter will give you guidance on how best to achieve this. Adopting a structured approach to your workload, notes and revision is essential.

ORGANISING YOUR NOTES

The easiest way to order your notes is by dividing them into sub-topics. This has been made easier for you by the SQA: lists of the Fields of Study and tables containing respective Key Issues can be found in the Advanced Higher History Course and Unit Support Notes on the SQA Advanced Higher page.

Field of study 1 – Northern Britain from the Iron Age to AD 1034

Key Issues	Description of Content of possible topics that could be covered
Iron Age/Celtic society	• Evidence: archaeological and literary • The nature of society: rural, hierarchical, tribal, familial • Importance of power and prestige • Belief systems: votive offerings, numinous places, cult of the head, sacrifices • Way of life: clothing, tools, crafts, weapons, diet, farming
Roman military invasions	• Flavian period • Pre-Agricolan contacts • Gask frontier • Agricola's five campaigns in Northern Britain • Tacitus' "The Agricola" • Battle of Mons Graupius • Flavian frontier • Hadrian's Wall: purposes and effectiveness • Antonine advance into Northern Britain • Antonine Wall: purposes and effectiveness • Comparisons of Hadrian's and Antonine Walls

It is vital that your notes are ordered so that they are easily accessible to you. You should buy a lever-arch folder, and a set of dividers with tabs and a cover page. Make sure these are extra-wide to allow the use of poly-pockets. Write each of the Key Issues sections onto a separate tab of your dividers. Then, behind each tab of Key Issues, you should have individual poly-pockets for the following: Revision Notes; Essays and Essay Plans; Source Work; Class Notes; Handouts. If you are handwriting notes for your dissertation, you may also want a separate section for this. Note that this process is easier if you use loose-leaf paper or a notepad to take notes in place of a jotter.

You want to be able to organise your notes in this thematic way so that you can come back to sections of the Key Issues more easily. Once you have found or have been provided with handouts and class notes, you will want to take your own notes on these (for guidance on note-taking, see the Dissertation chapter). After completing a section, you should then set about condensing these notes (for guidance on this, refer to the guide later in this chapter) to form revision notes that are more manageable and easier to revisit later in the year.

Preparing for the Question Paper: Organisation

ORGANISING YOUR REVISION

Where?

The most effective place for you is often dependent on where you can concentrate best, free from distractions. It should be a place where you are unlikely to be interrupted, with all of the materials and stationery that you need, so you don't need to break concentration.

Have a watch or clock nearby in order to be able to time your revision. If you are using a phone, tablet or computer, make sure you disconnect from social media to allow full concentration. Flight Mode is a useful feature to help you focus.

It has been found that attempts to remember information are much more successful when you are less stressed, you eat healthily and you exercise often.

When, and for how long?

You should avoid trying to revise when you are tired. You may be able to create revision materials when you are tired, but it is more effective to do this when you are alert, as creating these materials is a form of revision in itself, that helps you to form memories.

During a revision session, as time progresses, learning efficiency continues to deteriorate. This is particularly true when you have not set an end time. However, if you set a finishing time, for example after two hours, learning efficiency will deteriorate to begin with but improve again towards the end of the two hours. Taking short breaks of approximately five minutes within this time will help keep learning efficiency as high as possible. Thus, an effective revision session would consist of four 25-minute sessions interspersed with three five-minute breaks.

How often?

Your ability to recall the information you have just revised improves for the first 10 minutes after stopping, then begins to deteriorate as the days and weeks go by. So, how often should you re-visit the same information? If you quickly read over the material after 10 minutes, recall improves again, and similarly after 1 day; 1 week; then 4 weeks. Hence, reviewing this information at these intervals will help embed it in your memory.

This process needs to be repeated with all the information you need to learn. Consequently, you need to start revising as you receive the information, and this needs to be highly structured throughout the course.

 **DON'T FORGET**

It is essential that revision begins as soon as is practical, i.e. once you have finished studying the first of the Key Issues.

THINGS TO DO AND THINK ABOUT

Creating a Study Timetable

To revise effectively, use the following steps:
- Buy or create an annual academic wall planner: this will give you an overview of the whole year at a glance.
- Make a list of what information you need to learn for your Field of Study, including a list of the Key Issues.
- Ask your teacher when each of the sections of Key Issues will be covered. Then, write in when your initial revision of each section will take place (this should be as soon as possible after completing a section).
- Add in time that you will reserve for reviewing sections that you have previously revised, at the intervals specified above. You should aim to revisit each of these sections at least once per month after the initial four-week process. This will strengthen your memory of earlier topics in preparation for the Question Paper.
- Be mindful that you will have more revision sessions to complete towards the end of the academic year, as you amass more new information while revisiting old information. Try to space this out as much as possible during the week.
- You will also need to factor in time for revision of other subjects apart from History.

It is highly likely that your plans will slip as other events, illness or tiredness take over. Do not worry too much about this, as you can adapt your timetable to facilitate this; although this is one of the reasons why it is essential to have started to revise early in the year.

 ONLINE

To find advice and apps for planning a revision timetable on the SQA website, go to the link on our Digital Zone at www.brightredbooks.net/subjects

PREPARING FOR THE QUESTION PAPER
CONDENSING YOUR NOTES

By the end of the course, you will have amassed a significant number of notes. These will be too voluminous to allow for effective revision in their original state. The first stage of revision involves reducing these notes considerably. This process should be carried out as the teaching of each section of the Key Issues is completed.

Condensing your notes does not simply mean reducing the volume of information that you have for a given topic; instead, you should change its form, for instance, grouping related information together in a new way. Condensing your notes in this way will help you to create new memories of this information.

In principle, you should begin with a large volume of notes and aim to reduce this to a few sides of A4 for each section of the Key Issues. Towards the end of the course, you can aim to go further and have one sheet of A3 paper, which you can refer to in the days before the exam, that contains keywords and mnemonics that unlock the contents of the entire course in your mind.

In order to be able to identify the pertinent information required for completing the Question Paper, the starting point is again the Course and Unit Support Notes. It is essential that you build up a set of revision materials based on the Key Issues, using the Description of Content as further explanation of what could be asked.

OMITTING TOPICS TO REDUCE WORKLOAD

When referring to the Key Issues and Description of Content of a Field of Study, you will notice that some of the content is *italicised* and some is not. The italicised content is that which can be examined in the form of essay and/or source-handling questions. That which is not italicised can only be examined through essay questions. Consequently, due to there being a choice of essay questions, you may be tempted to sacrifice study of some or all sections that are not italicised. However, this is a risky tactic, as there are four such sections in each Field of Study. In having to write two essays from a choice of five, you may limit your choice severely, or indeed not be able to answer two questions confidently.

STRATEGIES FOR CONDENSING NOTES

The following strategies allow you to change the structure and form of your notes, as well as reducing their volume. This is not an exhaustive list, and how you choose to condense notes is very much down to personal style.

Flowcharts

1) Identify key events / themes to remember.

2) Put these in boxes one below the other.

3) At the right-hand side of each box, write down extra detail about that box.

4) Annotate with relevant Historical Sources and Interpretations.

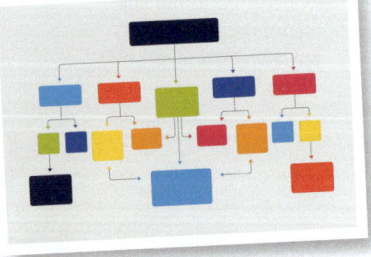

Mind maps

1) Identify groupings to remember.

2) Put the name of a group in a box drawn centrally on the paper.

3) In circles around the central box, put the main features of the group.

contd

Preparing for the Question Paper: Condensing Your Notes

4) Add detail to explain around each of the secondary boxes.

5) Annotate with relevant Historical Sources and Interpretations.

Flashcards

1) Write a question or the name of an event on one side of the card.

2) On the back, write the answer / details of event. Also add in Historical Sources and Interpretations.

3) Test yourself, or get others to test you.

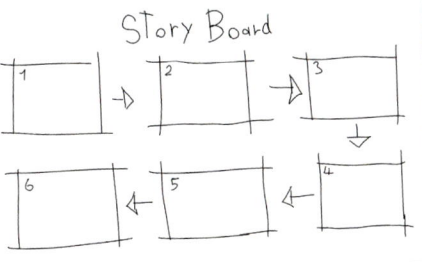

Storyboards

1) Summarise the story or process into main events or steps.

2) Create a blank storyboard / cartoon strip.

3) Write a short description of each event or step in each of the smaller boxes.

4) Draw an image of the event in each of the larger boxes above.

Placement

1) Identify main things you need to remember for a topic / subject, including Historical Sources and Interpretations.

2) Write on Post-Its – keep it brief so that you can read it easily – 4 or 5 words.

3) Stick these on a wall, and move them to different locations when you can remember each one.

4) After a few hours / days, check if you can expand on the information on a note – if not, move it back.

HISTORICAL SOURCES AND INTERPRETATIONS

Historians research the past by using available evidence to form opinions and ideas about historical issues. They often have different viewpoints and thoughts (interpretations) of what has happened.

You need to refer to relevant Historical Works, at least once in each essay, in order to be awarded higher than 12 from 25 marks. Hence, it is important to incorporate this into your revision notes.

- You may decide to have the names of historians linked to certain factors which lead to an event.
- Alternatively, you may decide to use the contrasting opinions of historians as the basis for the paragraphs of an essay. So, in your notes, link relevant knowledge to support the differing views.

 ONLINE

There is much more advice on how to condense your notes available, especially from Higher Education institutions. Check out the link at our Digital Zone: www.brightredbooks.net/subjects

 THINGS TO DO AND THINK ABOUT

You may be tempted to try to learn prepared answers to essay questions that may appear in the Question Paper. Avoid doing this, as the questions can have a particular focus that may differ from your predictions. A better approach is to identify areas of historical debate in the Key Issues.

PREPARING FOR THE QUESTION PAPER

REVIEW AND INFORMATION RETRIEVAL

The third step in the process of preparing for the exam is to re-visit your revision notes and employ techniques to help you remember information when sitting the exam.

REVIEWING YOUR NOTES

Reviewing your notes in its simplest form can mean spending a few minutes at the start of your next study session reading over what you learned previously. If you have not already identified keywords for each section of the Key Issues while condensing your notes, you should do so now. These are the words that provide headings for sections and subsections of your revision notes.

However, there are other techniques you could try:

- One of the most effective ways is to attempt Past Paper questions. This allows you to review key knowledge and to practise exam skills at the same time.
- You could attempt to re-create summaries of the main keywords on scrap paper.
- Put keywords on Post-Its and test how much you know about each one.
- You could try to explain what you have learned to someone else.

DON'T FORGET

The amount of information that you can recall from any initial revision session significantly depreciates after 24 hours. It is essential that you review this material the following day, then a week later, then four weeks later. Following that, it should then be reviewed on a monthly basis until the exam takes place.

RETRIEVING INFORMATION FROM MEMORY

As an additional layer of revision, you should apply techniques to your revision notes that will aid recall of information when sitting the exam. These techniques will help you organise groupings of keywords into more memorable forms. In the exam, you can then use these to unlock large amounts of information from your long-term memory.

Acronyms

Use these for remembering lists or groups of information.

1) Write down the grouping of keywords that you want to remember.
2) Take the first letter from each word.
3) Create a memorable word or combination of letters.

Example:

When trying to remember what the main driver / feature of Iron Age society was, from Field of Study 1: Northern Britain from the Iron Age to AD 1034, you could create an acronym.
Keywords
- Religion
- Agriculture
- Warfare / Militaristic
- Power

Remember this with the acronym **RAW Power**.

Acrostics

Use these for remembering lists in order and in groups.

1) Write down the grouping of keywords that you want to remember.
2) Take the first letter from each word.
3) Make up a memorable sentence, using the letters you have written down as the first letter of each word. They should be in order if it is a series of events.

Example:

When trying to remember the key reasons for Northern victory in the American Civil War, from Field of Study 4: USA: "A House Divided", 1850–1865, you could create a sentence from the following linked words:

Keywords	Sentence words	Keywords	Sentence words
Military	manage	Politics	preserve
Economy	every	Social	state

So, you would remember:
"The North won and managed to preserve every state"
to unlock the reasons for Northern victory.

contd

Rhyming

Use this for remembering groups and processes, in order:

1) Write down the grouping of keywords that you want to remember.
2) Create a rhyme or song containing these words.
3) This is more effective if it links to the reason why you are trying to remember the grouping. It could tell a story if trying to remember an order.

Example:

When trying to remember the key features of the instability of the Weimar Republic, 1918–1923, from Field of Study 6: Germany: From Democracy to Dictatorship, 1918-1939, you could make a rhyme such as the following.

Spartacists and the Left, Kapp, Hitler and the Right,
Versailles and hyperinflation affected Germany's economic might,
Suspicions of coalitions and assassinations galore,
No wonder the Weimar Republic ended up on the floor.

You can also summarise Historical Sources and Interpretations in this way. Here is an example of how to remember historians' opinions on why the Romans invaded Scotland, from Field of Study 1: Northern Britain from the Iron Age to AD 1034.

Why did the Romans come to Scotland at all?
Maxwell is sure that they wanted to conquer it all,
While Anthony Kamm thinks they wanted to expand,
And Breeze believes they wanted peace throughout the land.

ONLINE

Go to our Digital Zone at www.brightredbooks.net/subjects and click the link to a website that will generate memorable acrostics for you if you type in the first letter of each keyword.

Memory palace

Use this when trying to remember lists and processes, in order.

1) Write down the grouping of keywords that want to remember.
2) List the things you do on your way to school. Make sure you choose to list the same number of activities as you have keywords.
3) Link the first activity you complete on your way to school, to the first keyword on the list. Do this by thinking of the keyword when carrying out the activity, over a few days. Replicate this with the second, the third and so on.
4) Thinking of your actions on the way to school, while you are in the exam, will unlock the keywords in order.

Example:

When trying to remember the key features of Edward's invasion of Scotland in 1296, from Field of Study 2: Scotland, Independence and Kingship, 1249-1334, you could link the following:

	Activity	Key Event
1.	Pack school bag:	Siege of Berwick
2.	Lock the door:	Siege of Dunbar Castle
3.	Wait at bus stop:	Battle of Dunbar
4.	Sitting on bus:	Abdication of John
5.	Getting off the bus:	Removal of Stone of Destiny
6.	Walking into school:	Berwick Parliament

ONLINE

Use online tools to help you with creating rhymes, such as www.rhymer.com. There are also guides to retrieval techniques on many Higher Education sites - go to our Digital Zone at www.brightredbooks.net/subjects and check out the links there.

 THINGS TO DO AND THINK ABOUT

Although adding these techniques to your revision may seem that you have to remember more information, the reverse is true. Grouping information together in this way allows easier recall later. There is also the added benefit of having changed the nature of the information. This in itself aids the process of forming stronger long-term memories.

PREPARING FOR THE QUESTION PAPER

IN THE EXAM

By the end of the Question Paper, you will be expected to have completed two essays and three source questions. There are 90 marks available for the Paper, and you will be expected to achieve this in three hours.

CHOICE

Each Field of Study is set out in the same way with the same level of choice and difficulty. You should make your choice of what questions to complete from within one Field of Study only. Once you have found your Field of Study within the Paper, you will:

- be presented with five essay questions worth 25 marks each. From this list, you will choose two to complete.
- be presented with four sources and three source-handling questions. You will use all of the sources to complete the three questions. There is no choice here.

Before you start writing your answers, check that you fully understand what the question is asking. Read each question carefully and consider whether your initial assumptions about the question are correct and that you are aware of what the specific focus is.

TIMING

Having 180 minutes to achieve 90 marks means that you have two minutes per mark. Calculating in this way means this also includes reading and thinking time. Hence, you should aim to divide your time in the following manner:

Marks for a question	12 marks	16 marks	25 marks
Time to spend on it	24 mins	32 mins	50 mins

Essay questions

Spend 50 minutes on each of these. You should underline key words, quickly plan the essay and note down relevant historical sources and interpretations before you begin, giving you approximately 45 minutes of writing time.

contd

12-mark Source-handling questions

Spend 24 minutes on these. Highlight the issue in the question, read the source and highlight key interpretations. Leave approximately 20 minutes for writing. You may want to divide your time further here: for instance, it should take you just over five minutes to write about interpretations from the source.

16-mark Source-handling questions

You have 32 minutes to complete this question. Plan out your answer before you begin, leaving yourself with about 25 minutes of writing time.

It is unlikely that you will be able to keep strictly to these times. You may find that one Source is more difficult to understand, or an essay takes longer to write. However, it is essential that you track the time in the exam in order to avoid running out of time.

If a question is about a sub-topic that you know well, you may be tempted to spend more time on this in order to pick up maximum marks. However, there is a maximum number of marks for each question, so this is not the best strategy. Alternatively, if you find that you are struggling to write a great deal for one of the essays, you could divide the remaining time up among the other questions. This is not necessary for the source-handling questions though, as you should at least be able to identify Interpretation points and Source Content Provenance points.

APPROACH

Read over the instructions on the front page of the Question Paper. Use the Contents Page on Page 2 to locate the questions for your Field of Study. Then read over all questions once. Write down relevant keywords and historical sources and interpretations that come to mind for all of the questions, just in case you forget when under pressure later in the exam. Then make a decision on what essays you want to attempt.

It may be normal to approach the questions in the order that they appear, although this is not necessary. As long as you number each answer, you can attempt them in any order.

You may decide to attempt the questions you are more confident with first, allowing you to confidently answer in good time. In this way, you can then concentrate on more tricky questions last, with peace of mind that you will have already gained a considerable number of marks.

You may feel under a lot of pressure in the first few minutes and feel like you may panic. While looking at the questions for the first time, you may feel like you cannot remember anything. If this happens, take a few deep breaths and focus on something you can do. Read over the essay questions slowly, then read over the source-handling questions and the sources themselves. If you still feel under pressure, you may want to start with source-handling questions, as the beginnings of these answers are in front of you.

 **DON'T FORGET**

The time that is allocated for the exam includes reading and thinking time too, thus it is not necessary to be constantly writing. Take time to re-focus your thoughts before starting a new question.

 ONLINE

There are numerous helpful websites to help you mentally prepare for exams. If you know you suffer from anxiety and stress in or before exams, click the link to the NHS site at our Digital Zone: www.brightredbooks.net/subjects

 ## THINGS TO DO AND THINK ABOUT

If you know you are a person who suffers adversely from stress in exams, and you find it difficult to recall information that you knew before walking into the exam hall, you should prepare for this. Treat the exam as the final stage in a journey that starts with planning and preparation early in the course, and make sure you do regular revision throughout.

THE QUESTION PAPER, PART 1 – ESSAY QUESTIONS

THE NATURE OF THE ESSAY QUESTIONS

Part 1 of the exam consists of essay questions. You will be presented with five questions and will choose two of these to answer. The focus of the essay questions can be selected from any of the topics in the Key Issues, whether italicised or not.

ESSAY QUESTIONS FEATURES

Command words
These are the words that will tell you how to answer the question. They may ask you to validate or justify an opinion. Alternatively, they may ask you to weigh up historical information in causing or explaining events.

Historical Issue / Topic
This is the main focus of the question. It may be that you are asked about why an event happened, what the impact of a historical event was, or how influential a historical figure was.

Isolated Factor
Some questions may contain an Isolated Factor. This is an event or a concept that has a relationship with the topic of the question. You will be expected to provide information on this factor and explain how it has led to, or had an impact on, the topic. This will not be the only factor that influenced the topic of the question – you will be expected to discuss these Other Factors too, in order to make a considered judgement on the topic.

Example:

Command Words.　Isolated Factor.　Historical Issue / Topic.

To what extent did the promise of raiding opportunities attract the Vikings to Northern Britain?

In this case, the Historical Issue is what led the Vikings to attack then settle in Northern Britain. The Isolated Factor is opportunities to raid. The Command Words are asking you to weigh up the importance of the Isolated Factor in causing the Historical Issue. Hence you would discuss raiding as a cause of why the Vikings arrived in Northern Britain, but then should consider the relative importance of Other Factors such as the need for land; strategic importance for trade and exploration; or geographical similarities with Scandinavia. You should then make a judgement on how important the promise of raiding was in causing the Vikings' arrival.

WORDING OF THE QUESTION

Essay questions will contain varying Command Words. Some may provide a statement and then ask how justified the statement is, while others may ask the extent to which something is true. The Command Words can give you some guidance on how to structure your answer. Hence, do not be confused by essay questions that provide a quote and then ask a question, just because it may be more grammatically difficult to refer back to in the body of an essay.

Example:

"The route of instability in the early years of the Weimar Republic can be traced to the signing of the Treaty of Versailles."
How justified is this view?
It is important to realise that the same question could be thought of as the following:
To what extent was the signing of the Treaty of Versailles the route of instability during the early years of the Weimar Republic?
This does not change the aim of the question; it simply makes it easier to refer to in your answer. Be careful, if you want to reword a question in your mind, that you do not change its aim. This will lead you to losing marks, and it may result in your answer failing. Do not change a question without an Isolated Factor into one that has one, or vice versa.

THE TYPE OF ESSAY QUESTIONS

Essay questions can be asked in a variety of ways. Generally, they can be divided into ones with, and ones without Isolated Factors.

Questions with Isolated Factors

Essay questions may have Isolated Factors, asking you to evaluate the importance of the factor to the issue raised in the question. In this type of question, you should weigh up the importance of the Isolated Factor. This is often done by comparing its importance to that of Other Factors. You must address the Isolated Factor in order to pass.

Example:
These are examples of essay questions that contain Isolated Factors:
How far does propaganda explain the lack of opposition to Nazi rule between 1933-1939?
Here you would need to discuss the effects of propaganda in increasing Nazi popularity at the expense of others. You could then also discuss alternative explanations such as the disorganisation of opposition groups; the lack of evidence for disobedience and individualistic opposition; and/or the role of fear and intimidation in the Third Reich.
How far does Union military success explain why Europe remained neutral during the US Civil War?
For this essay, you would need to address how Northern military success affected European attitudes. However, you could also discuss the influence of economic factors; Northern and Southern diplomacy; and/or popular opinion in European countries.

Assessment Questions (Questions without an Isolated Factor)

Alternatively, they may ask you to make a judgement on a historical issue without considering an Isolated Factor. You are not expected to weigh up the importance of factors here. Instead, you should assess evidence that supports the view proposed in the question; then you should assess evidence that contradicts the view. You should not treat this as an Isolated Factor. However, when organising information for revision purposes, it is still useful to group related information together, like knowledge under a factor. You can then utilise a number of these groupings to help support, and then to oppose the view in the question, before coming to an overall judgement. That is, look to prove or disprove the view in the question, using a number of different groupings of information.

Example:
These are examples of essay questions that do not contain Isolated Factors:
How far is King John's negative reputation undeserved?
In this case, you would present information that suggests the view in the question is well founded, i.e. John was a more competent king than is generally believed. You would then be able to discuss why the view is somewhat unwarranted.
Stalin's policy of industrialisation had achieved its aims by 1941.
How justified is this view?
To answer this, you would firstly cite evidence to show industrialisation as effective. Then, you could tackle the other side of the argument, i.e. there were serious failings masked by propaganda.

DON'T FORGET
You should read and then re-read each essay question carefully in the exam. Identify the Command Words and the Historical Issue in the question. Then ask yourself if it contains an Isolated Factor before proceeding to write a plan. If an Isolated Factor is present, you must discuss this in your answer.

THINGS TO DO AND THINK ABOUT

Think about approaching each question by focusing specifically on what it is asking, and not by trying to change it to a question you have a ready-made answer to. Organise your revision notes into sets of information about an individual topic which you can employ to prove and disprove the Historical Issues.

ONLINE
Use the Past Papers and Marking Instructions on the SQA Advanced Higher page to practise identifying the individual features of questions. Go to our Digital Zone at www.brightredbooks.net/subjects to click the link there.

THE QUESTION PAPER, PART 1 – ESSAY QUESTIONS

MARKING CRITERIA AND STRUCTURING YOUR ESSAY

MARKING CRITERIA

There are no distinct marks awarded for Knowledge, Analysis, Evaluation or Structure. Instead, the mark an essay is given is based on four criteria, namely;

- Structure
- Thoroughness and/or Relevance of Information and Approach
- Analysis, Evaluation and Line of Argument
- Historical Sources and Interpretations

The marks that an essay is allocated correspond loosely to the grading below.

A++ – 23–25 marks   A+ – 20–22 marks

A – 18-19 marks   B – 15–17 marks

C – 13–14 marks   D – 10–12 marks

No Award – 0–9 marks

However, the marks in the essay section need to be combined with those gained in the source-handling section and the Dissertation component, before a Grade is assigned.

Weighting of criteria

There are two criteria that decide which range of marks, i.e. which grade, an essay will achieve. These are Thoroughness / Relevance of Information; and Approach and Analysis / Evaluation / Line of Argument. Then all of the criteria are used to allocate a specific mark within a range.

ONLINE

To further understand the standard expected for essay-writing, go to our Digital Zone at www.brightredbooks.net/subjects and click the link to refer to the General Marking Principles section of the Past Paper Marking Instructions. This document provides a grid that explains how the essays are judged.

STRUCTURING YOUR ANSWER

The approach you take to answering any given essay question is your own choice. How you decide to do this will be based on a number of factors:

- The type of question – an Isolated Factor question, or one that asks you to take measure of a historical issue.
- You may prefer a simple structure that deals with each side of the argument separately (the view presented in the question, then the opposing view).
- Alternatively, you may prefer to write thematically, discussing relevant features separately, and evaluating how much they support the view presented in the question.

HISTORICAL INTERPRETATIONS

For your essay to pass, it is essential that you include reference to the work of historians. Historians and their opinions can be introduced in a number of places in an essay. They can be inserted using the historian's name only, or with an opinion that is paraphrased, or indeed with a quote. Alternatively, you may mention a school of thought.

TAKING SIDES – SUPPORTING AND OPPOSING THE VIEW IN THE QUESTION

Remember that historians will have varying opinions on the Historical Issue that is asked about in the question.

The Question Paper, Part 1 – Essay Questions: Marking Criteria and Structuring Your Essay

Hence, there is always an opposing argument, or indeed set of arguments. Think of the answer to any essay question as having multiple possibilities:

- You could be supportive of the view presented in the question, discrediting other views.
- You could highlight how one factor (perhaps the Isolated Factor, but not necessarily) is more important than the others, or indeed a combination of factors.
- You could acknowledge that numerous views have merit.
- You could highlight how some developments / factors are caused or intensified by one particular development / factor.

In your answer, you should aim to present arguments, showing connections between them. In your conclusion, you should ultimately prioritise one.

If the question contains an Isolated Factor, this could be regarded as one side of the argument, in support of the question. You should dedicate a significant portion of your essay to discussing the Isolated Factor. It should also be discussed when you are evaluating the significance of Other Factors – a comparison of sorts should be made.

PRIORITISING IN AN ISOLATED FACTOR QUESTION

You may decide to agree with the view presented in the question, that the Isolated Factor is indeed the most significant factor. In this case, you should address the Isolated Factor first, writing as much as you can. In your Conclusion, you should answer the question on the basis that the Isolated Factor is the most significant factor.

If you decide that another Factor is more influential than the Isolated Factor, it is completely valid to argue this. In this case, you should again address the Isolated Factor first. Then you should address what you deem to be the most influential of the Other Factors. You can then present the rest of the Other Factors in declining order of importance. In your Conclusion, you should answer the question on the basis that the Isolated Factor is not the most significant, and that in fact Other Factors, and in particular one factor, are more significant.

 ONLINE

Use the Past Papers and Marking Instructions for each question - on the SQA Advanced Higher Page - to help you identify the aim of each question in your Field of Study. Consider the way that the Marking Instructions for each individual question are structured. They will show you appropriate ways to divide your answer into sections. You can then apply this thinking to questions you are asked to answer. Go to www.brightredbooks.net/subjects for more.

DON'T FORGET

You should present a directed and coherent line of argument throughout. This should begin in your introduction, evolve in the main body and naturally arise in the conclusion. The reader should not be surprised by the decision you make in your final Conclusion.

Questions with Isolated Factors

A simple structure for a question with an Isolated Factor. The section on the Evidence to oppose the Isolated Factor is optional, as is the number of Other Factors that you choose to discuss.

- Introduction
- Evidence and analysis to support the Isolated Factor in the question
- Evidence and analysis to oppose the Isolated Factor in the question
- Evidence and analysis to support Other Factors:
  • Other Factor 1
  • Other Factor 2
  • Other Factor 3
- Conclusion

This is a more evaluative approach to an Isolated Factor, allowing for a strong line of argument.

- Introduction
- Evidence and analysis to support the Isolated Factor in the question
- Evidence and analysis to oppose the Isolated Factor in the question
- Mini-Conclusion
- Evidence and analysis to support Other Factors:
  • Other Factor 1
  • Other Factor 2
  • Other Factor 3
- Mini-Conclusion
- Conclusion

Questions without Isolated Factors

A simple structure for a question without an Isolated Factor

- Introduction
- Evidence and analysis to support the view presented in the question
- Evidence and analysis to oppose the view presented in the question
- Conclusion

 THINGS TO DO AND THINK ABOUT

Test how much you know by using Past Papers and writing out plans for each of the essay questions in your Field of Study. This will help identify where your knowledge is lacking.

THE QUESTION PAPER, PART 1 – ESSAY QUESTIONS
STRUCTURE CRITERIA – INTRODUCTIONS

The Introduction is part of the Structure criteria which helps you to gain marks for your answer. The Introduction should give an indication of how you intend to answer the question. You should set the Historical Issue in context. You should also identify the different ways that historians interpret the issue, including any interpretation mentioned in the question. You should then briefly consider the strengths and weaknesses of these interpretations. Having prioritised these, you should then indicate what line of argument you will adopt, and why.

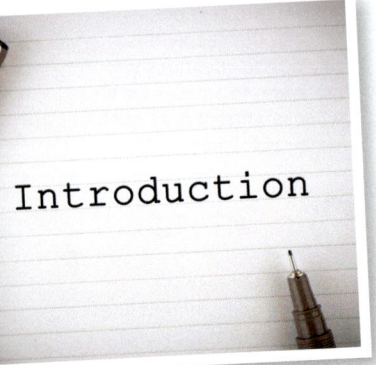

WRITING FRAME

Below is a sample structure that you could use. Remember that this is only one way that your Introduction may be structured. You may want to use it until you become more confident.

1) Contextualise the Historical Issue
2) Acknowledge any viewpoint presented in the question and explain this, including relevant Historical Interpretations
3) Present all other arguments including relevant Historical Interpretations
4) Indicate which interpretation / factor you will support
5) Explain briefly why it is more convincing than other views / factors.

Example:

Essay Question:
To what extent did the promise of raiding opportunities attract the Vikings to Northern Britain?

Sample Introduction:

The Vikings arrived in Britain as raiders, plundering remote monasteries, attacking Lindisfarne off the east coast in AD 793, while raiding Iona in the west two years later. A century later in AD 870, they laid siege to Dumbarton Rock under the leadership of Ivar the Boneless. The Anglo-Saxon Chronicle, the Irish Annals and Alcuin of York all lamented the violence of these invaders who seemed fixated on slaughter, looting and destruction. Both Downham and Walker suggest that the opportunity to raid did indeed attract the Vikings to Northern Britain, at least initially.

However, by the end of the ninth century, many Vikings had settled in Northern Britain, with the Western and Orkney Isles remaining under Scandinavian control well into the Medieval period.

contd

The Question Paper, Part 1 – Essay Questions: Structure Criteria – Introductions

In order to determine how significant the opportunities for raiding were in attracting the Vikings, we must also examine the possibility that it was a lack of land in Scandinavia, combined with the availability of arable farmland, in a more favourable climate, that encouraged migration. Ritchie discusses the importance of a desire for new land as being significant. Hence, it is possible to argue that although they may have initially sought out new places to plunder, it was the availability of land which became the main attraction for successive generations of Vikings.

Essay Question:
To what extent was the policy of a *Volksgemeinschaft* realised by the Nazis by 1939?
Sample Introduction:

After coming to power in 1933, the Nazis set about attempting to create a racially pure state whereby all German citizens would support the xenophobic and racist policies of the regime. They attempted to foster a productive and dedicated workforce, while protecting farmers and small businesses.

Moreover, they looked to promote traditional roles for women and exclude all 'non-Germans' from society. Meanwhile, they aimed to indoctrinate the youth of Germany with these ideas.

It could be argued that the Nazis were partially successful in achieving a Volksgemeinschaft, with both Evans and Kershaw highlighting that a racially pure state was achieved. However, others such as Stephenson are of the opinion that they were only partially successful. Kirk argues that support was coerced through fear, rather than given willingly.

Hence, it appears that a true Volksgemeinschaft was not realised by 1939.

 DON'T FORGET

It is essential that you include reference to Historical Works in your essay. The Introduction gives you an excellent opportunity to do this. Linking historians and schools of thought to the main interpretations will ensure that you surpass this expectation. Be mindful that you should include more Historical Sources and Interpretations in the main body of your essay.

 ONLINE

For further advice on writing effective introductions, refer to the Harvard Writing Centre by clicking on the link at our Digital Zone - www.brightredbook.net/subjects

 THINGS TO DO AND THINK ABOUT

There is a reason that each essay question is asked; it is alluding to an area of historical debate. In the introduction to your answer, it is your task to present this debate to the reader. A good way to approach this is to assume that the reader does not know the different arguments presented by historians, and to outline these briefly, before indicating why you have chosen to support one of these interpretations of the Historical Issue over another.

THE QUESTION PAPER, PART 1 – ESSAY QUESTIONS

CONSTRUCTING THE MAIN BODY OF YOUR ESSAY

The criteria most significant in deciding the grade that you are awarded for an essay are:
- Thoroughness and/or Relevance of Information and Approach
- Analysis, Evaluation and Line of Argument

THOROUGHNESS AND/OR RELEVANCE OF INFORMATION AND APPROACH

Your essay should show both "width" and "depth" of knowledge. For your essay to have a "width" means that it should present evidence linked to a variety of the main viewpoints and factors which relate to the topic. Indeed, you should cover as many of these as you can.

At the same time, having "depth" is important, as this is how you show the examiner how detailed your knowledge is. You could look to give as much detail about a single viewpoint or factor as possible. You should make sure that the evidence that you provide is analysed directly and is linked to your evaluation. Otherwise, your essay will be deemed to be too much of a narrative.

> **Example:**
> Essay Question: To what extent did the promise of raiding opportunities attract the Vikings to Northern Britain?
> To show a "width" of knowledge, you may want to discuss: over-population in Scandinavia and the need for land; the familiarity of the geographical features of the Northern British landscape; the desire to raid; the need for new trading partners; access to new sea routes.
> To show a "depth" of knowledge while discussing "the over-population in Scandinavia and the need for land", you could discuss:
> - why there was a lack of land
> - the effects of land shortage
> - the availability of land in Northern Britain
> - the quality of land in Northern Britain.

ANALYSIS, EVALUATION AND LINE OF ARGUMENT

In your answer to an essay question, you should focus on making a decision on the historical debate that is raised by the question – take a side and aim to support it throughout your essay.

Build your argument by analysing the significance of the Points of Knowledge that you make. Once you have presented this body of evidence relating to a factor/side of the argument, make evaluative points linking to the question. This could be in the form of a mini-conclusion.

Go on to analyse evidence that opposes your line of argument in subsequent paragraphs and evaluate these in the same way.

PARAGRAPH STRUCTURE AND WRITING FRAME

Below is one approach you could take to forming paragraphs in the main body of your essay. Following the structure below will help keep you focused on the question.

Analysis 1 (A1)	The first sentence in each paragraph should introduce the theme of that paragraph. This is sometimes called a topic sentence, or signposting. It should explain the argument or factor to be discussed in the paragraph, and explain how it links to the question. This could be a suitable place to introduce Historical Interpretations.
	All paragraphs following the first paragraph after the introduction should be connected to your line of argument. Thus, if the new paragraph supports the argument made in the Evaluation of the previous paragraph, you should begin with a supportive word (refer to the word bank opposite). If not, use appropriate wording to change stance on the argument.

contd

The Question Paper, Part 1 – Essay Questions: Constructing the Main Body of Your Essay

Knowledge and Understanding (KU)	The next section of your paragraph should provide factual information that helps support your argument or alternative interpretations. The amount that you write here is dependent on how much you know and how much time you have.
Analysis 2 (A2)	Write a sentence or two to explain why the factual information that you have just provided is relevant for supporting the theme of the paragraph. You should also explain the significance this has to the question.
Additional Knowledge and Analysis 2	Provide additional pieces of evidence to support the view(s) being made in this paragraph and explain their significance to the question.
Evaluation (E)	These final sentences should be reserved for holistically weighing up the importance of the theme, argument or factor that has been discussed in the paragraph. Hence, you should link what you have said to your overall argument. This should show consistency.

WORD BANK

The words below could be used as sentence-starters for different features of a paragraph.

A1 – Introducing an Important Interpretation

Most Important Interpretation (in your opinion)
- Above all ...
- Primarily ...

An Interpretation that Supports Evaluation in the Previous Section
- Furthermore ...
- Moreover ...
- Likewise ...

A1 – Changing Argument to an Alternative Interpretation
- However, ...
- Despite this ...
- Conversely ...

Follow this up with
- ... it is possible to argue ...
- ... it appears ...
- ... it could be suggested that ...

Knowledge – Introducing Additional Knowledge
- Furthermore ...
- Additionally ...
- Moreover ...

A2 – Analysing Knowledge
- This is important as ...
- This is significant because ...
- The implications of this ...
- As a result, ...
- This implies ...

E – Providing Evaluative Comment
- Hence ...
- Thus ...
- Subsequently

Follow this up with
- ... it is plausible to argue that ...
- ... it appears ...
- ... it is possible to deduce ...
- ... compared to ...

E – Weighing Importance
- Compared with ...
- Equally ...

Offering Opinion
- It would seem that ...
- It is possible...

BALANCED APPROACH TO ANALYSIS AND EVALUATION

You may want to discuss the importance of: a piece of evidence; a factor; or an argument and compare it to another. It is often more complicated than simply stating something "definitely is more important" or "isn't significant at all". This extreme approach tends to give the reader a rather bumpy read.

Rather, it is better for the flow of your essay to build your argument gradually. Here are ways to introduce analysis and evaluation in a more subtle way:

- This argument is more convincing because ...
- This argument carries less weight because ...
- This reinforces the belief that ...
- This lends more weight to the theory of ...
- This augments the argument that ...

 **DON'T FORGET**

You will gain credit for depth of knowledge as well as width when describing a Factor or aspect of the argument.

 ONLINE

Click the link at our Digital Zone (www.brightredbooks.net/subjects) for the SQA Understanding Standards website to see examples of essay paragraphs.

 THINGS TO DO AND THINK ABOUT

Assuming that you spend five minutes planning your answer and another five minutes each on the Introduction and Conclusion, you would have 35 minutes left for constructing the main body. In an essay without an Isolated Factor, you could spend 20 minutes writing about your chosen side of the argument and 15 minutes on the other side. In an Isolated Factor essay, you may choose to spend 15 minutes on that factor, then five to ten minutes each on Other Factors.

THE QUESTION PAPER, PART 1 – ESSAY QUESTIONS

HISTORICAL SOURCES AND INTERPRETATIONS CRITERIA

Providing comment on historical interpretations helps you to gain marks for your answer. It is essential that you do this at least once in each of your essays for them to achieve more than 12 of the 25 marks.

WHAT ARE HISTORICAL INTERPRETATIONS?

Historians research the past by using available evidence to form opinions and ideas about historical issues. They often have different viewpoints and thoughts (interpretations) of what has happened. The study of these interpretations is called historiography. Historians differ in their interpretations, as the issues surrounding events are not always certain. Moreover, there are often gaps in our knowledge of any given time period. Hence, when a historian presents an opinion, it is based on their interpretation of the evidence. Historians may differ in their opinions as a result of their own personal beliefs or their reading of a situation that is not entirely clear. Indeed, the people involved in historical events may have had a variety of motives for taking the actions that they did, making it difficult for historians to ascertain what these were.

HOW TO ACHIEVE HIGH CREDIT FOR HISTORICAL INTERPRETATIONS

Historical interpretations can be used either to add weight to an explanation you provide, or to add weight to your arguments and evaluation of the essay topic.

- In the most basic sense, historians and their opinions can be introduced to provide further knowledge or explain why knowledge is important.
- However, you will receive more credit if historians' views are used to introduce or support/oppose an argument.
- Responses will be highly credited if you discuss how historians' opinions vary and if you make connections between them. If you can, you should link historical interpretations together showing how some historians support each other's opinions, while others oppose them.
- The best responses will discuss the context of these views. This means that there will be an explanation of why historians made the comments / judgements that they did about an issue.
- Were these produced in a different time period to other interpretations of the topic?
- Were there significant external pressures on historians, writing in a specific time or place, to side with a specific interpretation?
- Do the comments/judgements belong to an opposing school of thought?
- Is there another reason why the author would take the view that he / she does?

WHERE IN YOUR ESSAY TO PLACE HISTORICAL INTERPRETATIONS

Here are some sensible places to insert Historical Interpretations:

- In the Introduction, to show support for different interpretations of the issue raised in the question.
- When introducing a new factor or line of argument, in the main body of the essay, in the first few sentences of a paragraph.
- When analysing or evaluating, in the main body of the essay. A particularly effective method is to use Historical Interpretations to support points of analysis or evaluation at the end of paragraphs.

Remember, you can also use them to be critical of the work of other historians.

contd

The Question Paper, Part 1 – Essay Questions: Historical Sources and Interpretations Criteria

Example:
Field of Study 8 – Russia: From Tsarism to Stalinism, 1914–1945
Historians influenced by political context:
Most Soviet historians did not deviate from a Marxist interpretation. This was understandable, as they were writing at a time when it seemed Communism was succeeding, and also when there was political pressure to support the ideology.

Example:
Field of Study 1 - Northern Britain from the Iron Age to AD 1034
Historians limited by evidence available:
Recent innovation in archaeological methodology has led to more accurate dating, preservation techniques and ways of discovering new evidence. Regarding the origin of the Scots, the traditional view, based on primary written evidence, was that they had migrated to Dal Riata from Ireland. However, there is now significant archaeological evidence, cited by historians such as Campbell and Foster, to suggest that the Scots were more likely indigenous to the British mainland.

WRITING FRAME

There are a number of methods for inserting historical interpretations into your essay. You can "name-drop" individual historians or schools of thought, paraphrase or quote. The following phrases could be used separately or in conjunction with one another:

- "_Many historians, such as_ [Author] _believe_ ..."
- "[Author] _believes that_ [Factor / Event] _is_ ..."
- "However, an alternative explanation is that ..."
- "_This is the view put forward by_ [Author], _who says_ [Quote]."
- "_They are supported by_ [Author]."
- "[School of Thought] _proposes that_ ..."
- "[Historian / School of Thought] _supports / opposes the view that_ ..."

Example:
Essay Question:
To what extent did the promise of raiding opportunities attract the Vikings to Northern Britain?
Sample points of comment on Historical Sources and Interpretations:

"Downham is of the opinion that the Vikings were initially attracted by the promise of new places to raid."

However, Owen suggests that "_much of the interior of the Scandinavian landmass was unsuitable for settlement, characterised by impassable barriers of high mountains, dense forests and deep bogs_", hence Vikings needed new lands to cultivate.

Example:
Essay Question:
To what extent was the policy of a _Volksgemeinschaft_ realised by the Nazis by 1939?
Sample points of comment on Historical Sources and Interpretations:

There is little support among historians for the Nazis fully achieving their aim of a _Volksgemeinschaft_. Historians such as Evans and Kershaw point to success in implementing racial policy, but not other aspects.

Peukert discusses the fact that opposition grew towards the Nazis in the 1930s, which brings into question whether the Nazis truly had the support of the people.

 **DON'T FORGET**

Historians often offer a specific interpretation of a historical issue. This does not make them right. These are interpretations and should be treated as such. Hence, if there is a good reason to, such as the view being outdated or largely disproven, acknowledge the opinion but then take issue with it. At the same time, all views put forward by prominent historians are respected now, or were at some point. It is therefore important to acknowledge them in your essay, but then you can look to challenge them.

 ONLINE

On the SQA Advanced Higher site, there are Past Paper questions and the detailed Marking Instructions for each question. At the end of each question's marking instructions is a list of prominent historians and their interpretations of the Historical Issue. Use these to build up a picture of where the arguments lie in your chosen Field of Study. You will find links on our Digital Zone - www.brightredbook.net/subjects

 THINGS TO DO AND THINK ABOUT

It is much better practice to include historical interpretation within the natural flow of your writing, as you build your argument through analysis and evaluation, rather than adding it in artificially at the end. It is important that, before you start writing your answer, you are already planning ahead to where you will use it. Make sure that before you begin you make a plan, annotating the main interpretations with historians who support these. This will act as a prompt for you to insert historians' views naturally.

THE QUESTION PAPER, PART 1 – ESSAY QUESTIONS

STRUCTURE CRITERIA – MINI-CONCLUSIONS AND CONCLUSIONS

The conclusion is part of the Structure Criteria which help you to gain marks for your answer. You must finish your essay with a formal conclusion. Although there are no specific marks allocated, failure to do this will affect your overall mark considerably. Without a conclusion, there would be no concrete way to judge what your final thinking was about the issue. This could lead to your essay being judged to have a weak line of argument and/or understanding of the issue.

MAIN CONCLUSION

The conclusion needs to provide an overall judgement. It is not good enough to simply support both sides of the argument and leave it there. You must decide which side is more convincing. You must bring your key arguments on both sides of the issue together here and form a final decision on why one side is more convincing than the other. Your key arguments should be taken from the main body of your essay. This is an appropriate place to bring in the arguments of prominent historians, and a place where you can support one school of thought over another.

Writing frame

Below is a sample structure that you could use. Remember that this is only one way that your conclusion may be structured. You may want to use it until you become more confident.

1) Make an overall judgement on the question.

2) Acknowledge the value of the side(s) of the argument that you have not favoured. Remember to provide reasons why you think this.

3) Now make your main argument for why you have made your decision on the question. This should be drawn from points of evaluation already made.

4) Discuss the main historical interpretations, and link these to your argument.

5) Restate your overall judgement on the question.

MINI-CONCLUSIONS

A mini-conclusion is a short paragraph that serves the function of summing up a section of your essay. These are not essential, but they do help you keep track of your thoughts. They are also useful if you happen to unexpectedly run out of time during the exam and fail to write a formal conclusion for your second essay. This should summarise the main arguments that you have made thus far and should only address one side of the argument.

The most appropriate place for a mini-conclusion is directly after you have finished discussing the first side of the argument, i.e. after the Isolated Factor if there is one, or alternatively after supporting the view presented in the question.

Another place that you may find this useful is before your main Conclusion when answering an Isolated Factor Question. This would serve to summarise why the Other Factors you have discussed are significant as a whole, i.e. this would consolidate your argument against the main factor.

If you decide to use this feature, be mindful of time.

 **DON'T FORGET**

The judgement that you make in the conclusion should not be surprising to the reader. It should arise logically from the evaluation made throughout your essay.

 ONLINE

For further advice on writing effective conclusions, refer to the Harvard Writing Centre by clicking the link on our Digital Zone – www.brightredbooks.net/subjects

 THINGS TO DO AND THINK ABOUT

When you are considering how to make a judgement on an essay question, ask yourself why one side of the argument is more convincing than the other. Is it that more prominent historians have made more convincing arguments? Would one side of the argument not be as significant without the influence of the other? Is one factor more severe than the others, or does it cause the other factors to develop? You must find convincing reasoning for choosing one side of the argument, or one factor, over the other(s), while taking care to explain your thinking.

THE QUESTION PAPER, PART 2 – SOURCE-HANDLING QUESTIONS

QUESTION TYPES AND AN EXPLANATION OF COMPONENTS OF SOURCE-HANDLING QUESTIONS

Part 2 of the exam consists of Source-Handling questions. You will be presented with four sources and three source-handling questions in the exam. These sources will normally be written, but can also be an image or a diagram.

QUESTION TYPES

There are three types of source-handling questions in the exam:

- The "Evaluate the usefulness ..." question
- The "How fully ...?" or "How much ...?" question
- The "Interpretation of Two Sources" question

COMPONENTS OF SOURCE-HANDLING QUESTIONS

You will need to consider a number of components of a source or sources depending on which question type you are tackling. There is a description of each of these components below.

COMPONENT 1 – SOURCE RUBRIC PROVENANCE

What is Source Rubric Provenance?
The rubric is the written detail given above the source itself. The provenance of a source is its origins: in other words, it refers to the author or producer of the source; the date that it was produced; the reasons behind production; and the type of source that it is.

How do I write about this?
You can approach this aspect in a similar way to how you would have answered the "*origin and possible purpose of the source*" part of the "Evaluate the usefulness ..." question in the Higher History paper. To gain marks for this aspect, you should evaluate the origins of the source in terms of the issue raised in the question. This means that to gain one mark, you need to indicate a part of the provenance that is significant, such as the author. You should then explain why it is significant to a historian researching the issue in the question. This explanation needs to explicitly link to the issue in the question, and explain why the provenance is relevant to a historian who is exploring this issue.

COMPONENT 2 – INTERPRETATION / SOURCE CONTENT PROVENANCE

What is Interpretation / Source Content Provenance?
To interpret a body of text, or an image, is to understand and then present its meaning. You will select relevant content from the source and present it as quotations or paraphrasing in your answer. If the source is pictorial, you will describe what you see. You will then need to explain its significance to the issue presented in the question.

contd

How do I write about this?
You can think of approaching this aspect in a similar way to how you would have answered the "*content of the source*" part of the "Evaluate the usefulness …" question in the Higher History paper. You should quote or paraphrase sections of the source. Then, you should explain why the piece of evidence is significant to a historian researching the issue in the question. This explanation needs to explicitly link to the issue.

It is possible that you will have to evidence a large portion of the source to provide a relevant interpretation. However, it is not wise to quote such a length of text; in this instance, it will be a more efficient use of your time to paraphrase. It is not recommended that you shorten a quote.

COMPONENT 3 – CONTEXTUAL DEVELOPMENT AND WIDER CONTEXTUAL DEVELOPMENT

What are Contextual Development and Wider Contextual Development?
You can gain marks in this section in a number of ways:
- **Contextual Development** is when you develop points selected from the source further, by providing your own knowledge.
- **Wider Contextual Development** is giving more points from your own knowledge that
  - details more information omitted by the source about the historical issue or event
  - provides different interpretations of the historical event or issue raised in the question.
- **Additional Historical Interpretations** – two marks can be gained for Historical Interpretations (see Component 4 below) in each source-handling question. However, additional marks (beyond the 2 specifically allocated for component 4) can also be gained for this component, up to the maximum mark allocation for Wider Conceptual Development.

In all instances, the information you provide from your own knowledge must be explained in terms of the issue raised in the question.

How do I write about this?
You can think of approaching this aspect in a similar way to how you would have answered the "*your own knowledge*" part of the "Evaluate the usefulness …" question in the Higher History paper. You can gain marks by providing further development of relevant Interpretations / Content Provenance points from the source by expanding on the detail given. You can also gain marks for detailing omissions which help answer the issue raised in the question.

Wider Contextual Development can also include details of Historical Interpretations, i.e. you could include five relevant Historical Interpretations in your answer. In this case, you would receive two marks for Historical Interpretations and a further three marks for Wider Contextual Development.

COMPONENT 4 – HISTORICAL INTERPRETATIONS

What are Historical Interpretations?
Many historical issues are hotly debated, and historians have different views on why and how events unfolded, as well as on the impact of these events. Often, these views can be grouped into "schools of thought".

How do I write about this?
You will be awarded marks here for linking historians' views to the view(s) represented in the source. These can be supporting a view in the source, or can provide an alternative standpoint on the view. This needs to be specific, though: referring to a historian's name with no real detail of their opinion of the issue in the question is unlikely to gain a mark.

 THINGS TO DO AND THINK ABOUT

Not all aspects of source-handling questions are examined in each of the questions. Use the question-specific guides on the following pages to identify what aspects need to be discussed when tackling each specific question-type.

 **DON'T FORGET**

When tackling the Source Content Provenance or Interpretations component of the source-handling question, there is no one set way that you are expected to do this. You can describe the interpretation fully in your own words, you can directly quote, or you can paraphrase. A combination of these approaches is acceptable.

 **DON'T FORGET**

It is permitted to quote from the source to gain a Source Content Provenance or Interpretation mark. However, if doing this, you **must** interpret the meaning behind the quote, i.e. explain how it is relevant to the issue in the question. You will not gain a mark if you fail to do this.

 ONLINE

For examples of source-handling questions, visit either the SQA Advanced Higher History webpage and click on the "Specimen Question Paper and Marking Instructions" link, or visit the Past Papers section of the SQA website. The Understanding Standards site will also provide you with worked examples. You can find links on our Digital Zone – www.brightredbooks.net/subjects

THE QUESTION PAPER, PART 2 – SOURCE-HANDLING QUESTIONS

THE "EVALUATE THE USEFULNESS ..." QUESTION

There will be one question of this type to answer in your Field of Study. It is worth 12 marks. The focus of this question is to decide about how useful the source is to a historian who is researching the issue or event raised in the question.

PROVENANCE

You are expected to evaluate the roots of the source, commenting on its origins and production. You should then interpret the content of the source to determine the view of the source. While providing analytical comment on these separate aspects, it is essential to show you are aware of the effect of the provenance on the source and how its usefulness is affected by this. You should then also place the source within its historical context to show how useful it is in detailing the issue raised in the question. Additionally, there are marks available for detailing historical interpretations that are related to the issue raised in the question. Hence all four components of source-handling questions are to be discussed in your answer:

- Source Rubric Provenance
- Source Content Provenance
- Contextual and Wider Contextual Development
- Historical Interpretations

ALLOCATION OF MARKS

The 12 marks available for this question will be awarded as follows:

Source Rubric Provenance	3 marks
Source Content Provenance	3 marks
Contextual and Wider Contextual Development	4 marks (which can include details of relevant Historical Interpretations)
Historical Interpretations	2 marks

ANSWERING THE QUESTION

This Question Type will always begin with: "Evaluate the usefulness of ... as evidence of ...".

Although in the National 5 Question Paper this type of question demanded that you use a more rigid formula for gaining marks, this is not the case at Advanced Higher level. Hence, there is no need to begin each sentence with "The [aspect] of the source is useful because ...". You are permitted to use varying language.

However, it is important to refer regularly to the issue raised in the question in order to keep yourself focused, and to make it clear to the marker why you have selected certain information to present. That being said, the essence of the question is the same as at Higher, so you can use a similar approach in terms of structuring the answer and use of language.

Source Rubric Provenance

When referring to the author, it is important at Advanced Higher level to explain the author's relationship with the opinion in the source and with the issue raised in the question, i.e. directly relate the provenance to the issue.

At this level, it is no longer enough to state, for example, that the author was knowledgeable about the issue.

You must explain in detail why this is:

- Ask yourself if the author is best placed to give details about the issue or event in the question.
- Ask yourself how the background of the author may colour his or her opinion of the issue or event in the question.

In light of this, you must then explain the extent of usefulness of the whole source to a historian who is researching the issue or event. Avoid using rehearsed reasons for provenance being useful, and instead link your statements directly to the question.

Meanwhile, when discussing the Timing of a source, it is necessary to place the source in context, i.e. explain why this timing is relevant to the issue in the question. This needs to go further than simply evaluating timing by saying that the author was, for example, an eye-witness. Provide comment on the time of production by linking relevant events at the time to the issue in the question, explaining its context and how this may colour the contents of the source. You must then again explain why

contd

this would be useful or detrimental to a historian who is researching the issue.

At the same time, when commenting on the Purpose of the source, it is again necessary to explain why the reasons for producing a source is important to what the question is asking.

- Is the source produced in response to events, or to provoke a response?
- Is it a by-product of events, or is it to record events?

Once the reason for production is deduced, you must then think of the implications of this for historians researching the issue in the question, and comment on the source's subsequent usefulness, or lack of it. You can no longer gain marks by, for example, stating that a newspaper was designed to inform public opinion. If it is a newspaper article, then discuss the intent behind the publication, and place it in context.

Source Content Provenance

When looking for content from a written source to interpret, it is normal that in any given source there will be three separate points that could be selected. These will often vary in length from short phrases and partial lines, to full sentences and paragraphs. Alternatively, it is possible that a pictorial source or image will be provided for you to interpret. If this is the case, again there should be three separate features to consider. You must interpret the picture and describe what you see. Content which you select from the source, whether written or pictorial, must be evaluated for its usefulness. Explain on a point-by-point basis why this would be useful (or not) to a historian who is researching the issue.

Contextual Development and Wider Contextual Development

When evaluating the usefulness of the source to a historian, providing wider contextual development is important, as it explains what the source does not. This provides a fuller picture of the issue being asked about. Thus, if the source is missing key details regarding the issue raised in the question, its usefulness is limited.

So, you should give additional information to further develop events and ideas mentioned in the source. Alternatively, you can introduce information that the source does not even allude to, as long as it is relevant to the historical issue in the question.

You must then explain why this information is important to the issue. Also realise that the source is limited in its usefulness, as it has not provided this information.

You can also gain marks for Historical Interpretations in this section, beyond the two marks specifically allocated for this.

Historical Interpretations

The opinions of historians can provide further contextualisation, support for, or opposition to both the provenance and the opinion of the source. When giving details of historians' opinions, they must be explicitly linked to the issue raised in the question.

 ### THINGS TO DO AND THINK ABOUT

It is important to remember that this type of question is asking about the "usefulness" of a historical source. Instead of viewing the source as a plain body of text, try to imagine it as an authentic historical document or artefact, whether that be a diary, a newspaper article, a government document, a treaty or a book. Then, bear in mind that you are being asked how useful this would be to a person – a historian – researching the issue in the question. Approach the question in this way when you evaluate whether the source is useful, in terms of its origins, its contents and its limitations.

 ONLINE

Visit the SQA Understanding Standards website for Advanced Higher History for annotated examples of 'Evaluate the usefulness ...' answers. You can find links on our Digital Zone - www.brightredbook.net/subjects

 DON'T FORGET

You have approximately 25 minutes to complete this question.

THE QUESTION PAPER, PART 2 – SOURCE-HANDLING QUESTIONS

WRITING YOUR ANSWER TO THE "EVALUATE THE USEFULNESS ..." QUESTION

Identify the keywords in the question, i.e. the Issue that the question is asking you about. Highlight these. It is good practice to briefly plan out your answer before you read the source. Annotate the Rubric Provenance with your thoughts on the usefulness of these details. Then, quickly note down key features of the issue of the question and any Historical Interpretations you can remember.

READING THE SOURCE

- Make sure that you read the correct source.

- Read the information above the Source and identify who wrote / produced it, the date of production, what type of source it is and any other information which may give you an indication of why it was produced.

- Read over the Source once, without stopping, to familiarise yourself with the content.

- Re-read the Source for understanding. Read it more carefully this time, making sure you understand the meaning of each sentence and any links there are to the issue in the question.

- Read the Source once more, this time highlighting or underlining the phrases, sentences or paragraphs which relate to the issue in the question. There should be three distinct points that can be selected for Source Content Provenance marks within each source.

WRITING FRAME

Below is a sample structure that you could use. Remember that this is only one way that your answer may be structured. You may want to use it until you become more comfortable with the aspects required for this question and how they should be focused towards the question.

1) Start by writing: "*The Source is useful for researching* [Issue in the Question]".

2) **Source Rubric Provenance** (3 marks)

    i. Write: "*The origin of the Source is useful for researching* [Issue in the Question] *because ...*", then discuss why the AUTHOR, the TIMING and the PURPOSE are useful for researching the issue in the question.

3) **Source Content Provenance** (3 marks)

    i. Identify one piece of information from the source.

    ii. Start by writing: "*The Source is useful for researching* [Issue in the Question] *because it explains / mentions / highlights / shows that ...*", then give details of one point of relevant information explained in the Source.

    iii. Write: "*This is useful to a historian researching* [Issue in the Question] *because it shows / is written to / is key to / is an important feature of / means that ...*", then explain why the Interpretation is relevant to the issue in the question.

COMPLETE THIS PROCESS TWICE MORE

contd

4) **Contextual Development and Wider Contextual Development** (4 marks)
   i. Develop information from the source further – Start by writing: "**This source mentions** [detail from source]. **This was ... / This suggests ... / This was because ... / This was when ...**"

OR

   i. Show information is missing – Start by writing: "**However, the Source is limited for researching** [issue in the question] **as it does not fully explain ... / it does not explain ... / it does not show ... / it does not provide information about ...**", then give details that further explain points in the source or provide omissions.

THEN

   ii. You must then explain why the information you have provided is useful. Write: "**This is useful to a historian researching** [issue in the question] **because it shows / is key to / is an important feature of /means that ...**, then explain why the information omitted from the source is relevant to the issue in the question.

COMPLETE THIS PROCESS THREE MORE TIMES

   Additionally, in place of some of the above points, you could discuss Historical Interpretations.

Historical Interpretations (2 marks)

Refer to historians and their views which relate specifically to the issue in the question. There are a number of ways you can do this:

- "[Other Author] **believes ... about** [issue in the question]."
- "[Source's View] **is a common opinion on this issue, as** [Other Author] **also agrees, saying that ...**"
- "[Source's View] **is a controversial opinion on this issue, as** [Other Author] **disagrees, and puts forward the view that ...**"
- You don't need to quote here but can paraphrase, or simply explain other historians' opinion on the issue.

GIVE TWO INTERPRETATIONS

CHECKING YOUR ANSWER

Read over your answer, checking that it makes sense and that no points or sections remain unfinished. Make sure that you have:

1) provided three comments on the Source Rubric Provenance, each with explanations of why they are useful to researching the issue
2) provided three points of Source Content Provenance, each with explanations of why they are useful in revealing the issue
3) provided four points of Wider Contextual Development, in the form of information omitted by the source or Historical Interpretations, and you have explained why each of these is relevant to the issue
4) included two other Historical Interpretations for full marks.

DON'T FORGET

This question asks you to focus on how useful the source is to someone researching the issue. You should analyse the points you make with this in mind.

 THINGS TO DO AND THINK ABOUT

In the early stages of learning how to construct your answers to this type of question, use the writing frame. You may want to create a mnemonic or acrostic memorable to yourself, to help you remember each aspect that you have to talk about. Then practise these questions with only this in mind. You can return to the frame if you are unsure.

31

THE QUESTION PAPER, PART 2 – SOURCE-HANDLING QUESTIONS

ALTERNATIVE STRUCTURES FOR THE "EVALUATE THE USEFULNESS …" QUESTION

A VARIETY OF APPROACHES

There is no particular way that you are expected to structure your answer. Below are some examples of alternative ways that you can do this. Each will allow you to gain full marks. An extended point can gain you four marks in the following way:

This structure is simplistic and allows you to deal with each aspect separately, making it more straightforward for you to easily review the number of points you have written about for each aspect.

This more complex structure allows you to develop the Source Content Provenance with Wider Conceptual Development (WCD) on a point-by-point basis. This is useful if the source is full of distinct points that can be developed in their own right. If you choose this, there is no need to develop every piece of Source Content Provenance in this way. You can pick and choose.

Structure 1:
- **Source Content Point** — Select information from the source and explain its usefulness to a study of the issue in the question.
- **Contextual Development (Further Development of interpretation)** — Develop Source Content Point further using your own knowledge.
- **Wider Contextual Development (Omissions)** — Give further information that the source doesn't mention.
- **Historical Interpretations** — Provide details of historians' opinions / schools of thought which directly relate to the interpretation.

Structure 2:
- Provenance
- Interpretation of Source
- Wider Contextual Development (Further Development of Points from Source) (Omissions) (Historical Interpretations)
- Historical Interpretations

Structure 3:
- Provenance
- 1st Interpretation of Source
- Wider Contextual Development (Further Development of Interpretation)
- 2nd Interpretation of Source
- Wider Contextual Development (Further Development of Interpretation)
- 3rd Interpretation of Source
- Wider Contextual Development (Further Development of Interpretation)
- Wider Contextual Development (Omissions) (Historical Interpretations)
- Historical Interpretations

SAMPLE QUESTION

Source A from *The Chronicle of the Scottish Nation* by John of Fordun, written after 1350:

Macduff appealed to the King of England, as, in his opinion, King John had shown too much favour to his accusers. He managed to have King John summoned to the English King's parliament in London. John accordingly appeared in person and decided that he would answer through a proxy, after discussing the matter with his council. When John was called and appeared in court by proxy, the King of England would not listen to John's proxy until the King of Scotland, who was sitting beside the King of England, rose from his place and stood in court before him, imparting his answers to his proxy with his own lips. John fulfilled these commands; and, having undergone these insults and slights against his kingly rank and dignity, he at length imparted his answers to his proxy. He returned home greatly crestfallen. So, he straightaway appointed a parliament and informed them of the insults, slights, contempt and shame which he had endured. He then strove, by all means in his small measure of power, to find some offset against the King Edward's wickedness. It was determined that King John should utterly recall the homage and fealty he had given to the King of England … and that he could no longer obey his commands at all.

Evaluate the usefulness of **Source A** as evidence of strains in King John's relationship with Edward I over John's legal right to govern Scotland. **12**

EXAMPLE ANSWER

The time of production gives us an indication of the usefulness of the source, as, being produced in the mid-1300s, it attempts to portray earlier events in such a way as to promote the Bruce dynasty against other claims to the Scottish throne. Hence, John of Fordun's chronicle may portray King John as a weaker king in order to show the weakness of the Balliol/Comyn factions, and to enhance the memory of King Robert I and his descendants. This may suggest a bias in the source which colours how the relationship between Balliol and Edward is portrayed. On the other hand, this section of the chronicle is seen as a reliable account of events, so much so that it has been used as a basis by others for writing a history of the Scots. It has been found to be based on numerous primary sources, which are now unavailable to us, and hence can be seen as a reliable account of the relationship between the two kings. [Two marks for Source Rubric Provenance]

The source is also useful as it provides explanation of why King John's relationship with Edward I was strained. It describes how "Macduff appealed to the King of England" and "he managed to have King John summoned to the English King's parliament in London". This illustrates that Edward had no respect for John's position as the head of his country and hence as the supreme judge in legal matters of Scotland. This shows conflict in their relationship. [One mark for Source Content Provenance] The source shows further strains in the relationship as it describes how John tried to answer questions in court via his proxy, but that Edward refused to acknowledge the proxy until John had got up from his seat beside Edward and given the answers to his proxy for all to see. This shows that the relationship was strained as John is humiliated in public by Edward, who again refuses to acknowledge John's position and his right to make a final judgement on Scottish legal cases. [One mark for Source Content Provenance] The Source is also useful in showing the impact that this treatment had on John as it explains that he "straightaway appointed a parliament and informed them of the insults, slights, contempt and shame which he had endured. He then strove, by all means in his small measure of power, to find some offset against the King Edward's wickedness." This suggests that John was extremely frustrated with Edward, enough to look for a way to take some revenge or look for a way to mitigate the wrongs that he believed were being done to him. This shows a strained relationship. [One mark for Source Content Provenance] The source is also useful as it briefly mentions the homage that John had paid to Edward, but it does not fully explain it. John had paid homage to Edward in the summer of 1292 during the Great Cause. This was fealty exacted from all of the competitors to the Scottish throne in return for them being accepted by Edward as true claimants. The fact that John was one of the last claimants to do this suggests his reluctance and alludes to a strained relationship from the start. [One mark for WCD]

However, the source is limited in its usefulness as it does not fully explain the difficulties in John's relationship with Edward. John swore fealty for the Kingdom of Scotland in November 1292 and paid homage once more on 26 December 1292 at Newcastle. He was to renew his homage to Edward during the Macduff case. This shows a relationship whereby Edward imposed his will and consistently dominated affairs between the two kings, with John struggling to gain a foothold, putting him under much strain. [One mark for WCD] This view of the relationship is suggested by Barrow, who is of the opinion that Edward I wanted to exercise his right as John's overlord publicly. [One mark for Historical Interpretations] Furthermore, the source does not explain the attempts John made to assert his right to make a final judgement on the Macduff case. He had ignored a previous summons to Westminster for Macduff's appeal against his judgement, showing a strained relationship with Edward. [One mark for WCD] After a second summons, John attempted to avoid questions by saying he could not answer without consulting his advisers and government officials. However, Edward threatened to place him in contempt of court and confiscate Scottish castles as punishment, so John acquiesced. This shows how the source is again limited in its usefulness, as it omits important details that show John being intimidated by Edward, which would have put a strain on the relationship. [One mark for WCD] Michael Penman believes that John was a weaker character than Edward, and this is why the relationship developed to John's detriment. [One mark for Historical Interpretations] The source also omits to mention that this was not the first occasion where Edward had ignored John's position as supreme judge of Scottish legal affairs. He had heard an appeal of a merchant of Berwick at his parliament in Newcastle, in December 1292. This forced John to alter the verdict in favour of the merchant. This would have created a strain in their relationship, as it made clear to John that Edward was willing to disregard John's position as King of Scotland. [One mark for WCD]

THINGS TO DO AND THINK ABOUT

You should make the effort to attempt as many sample or past exam papers as you can, to practise using these alternative answer structures.

THE QUESTION PAPER, PART 2 – SOURCE-HANDLING QUESTIONS

THE "HOW FULLY …?" QUESTION AND HOW TO ANSWER IT

THE QUESTION STEM

There will be one question, of this type, to answer in your chosen Field. It is also worth 12 marks. The focus of this question is to determine the extent to which the source illustrates the issue raised in the question. You should also place the source within its historical context to illustrate how much it reveals about the issue raised in the question. Additionally, there are marks available for providing valid historical interpretations. Thus, three components of source-handling questions need to be discussed for this answer:

- Interpretation
- Historical Interpretations
- Contextual and Wider Contextual Development

ONLINE

Visit the SQA Understanding Standards website for Advanced Higher History for annotated examples of "How fully …?" answers. You can find links on our Digital Zone - www.brightredbooks.net/subjects

ALLOCATION OF MARKS

The 12 marks available for this question will be awarded as follows:

Interpretation	3 marks
Contextual and Wider Contextual Development	7 marks (which can include details of relevant Historical Interpretations)
Historical Interpretations	2 marks

ANSWERING THE QUESTION

This Question Type will always begin with: "How fully does … explain …?" OR "How much …?"

Make a Judgement
You should make a judgement on the extent to which the source explains the issue in the question. The source will never explain the issue fully.

Interpretation
There will be three separate points or features that could be selected. Content which you select from the source, whether written or pictorial, must be explained in terms of its relationship to the issue in the question.

Contextual Development and Wider Contextual Development
The aim of providing wider contextual development here is to reveal the fullest picture of the issue that you can. Thus, if you can give further details of points raised in the source, or if the source is missing key details regarding the issue raised in the question, you mention them here, explaining their importance to the question. More discussion of Historical Interpretations can also be added here.

Historical Interpretations
The opinions of historians can provide further contextualisation, support for, or opposition to ideas expressed in the source. Again, these must explicitly relate to the issue raised in the question.

DON'T FORGET
You have approximately 25 minutes to complete this question.

DON'T FORGET
The Source will never explain the issue of the question in full. Think of the issue like a jigsaw puzzle with pieces missing. The Source represents the pieces that you have, and you must provide the missing pieces using your own knowledge.

WRITING YOUR ANSWER TO THE "HOW FULLY …?" QUESTION

Identify the issue that the question is asking you about. Then, before you read the source, briefly plan out your answer. Quickly note down key features of the issue in the question and any Historical Interpretations relevant to the issue in the question.

The Question Paper, Part 2 – Source-Handling Questions: Question Types ...

READING THE SOURCE

- Read over the Source once, without stopping, to familiarise yourself with the content.
- Re-read the Source for understanding. Read it more carefully this time, making sure you understand the meaning of each sentence and any links there are to the issue in the question.
- Read the Source once more, this time highlighting or underlining the phrases, sentences or paragraphs which relate to the issue.

WRITING FRAME

Below is a sample structure that you could use. Remember that this is only one way that your answer may be structured. Use it as a guide to help you in the first few attempts at these types of questions, and vary the layout once you become more confident.

1) Start by writing: "**The source explains** [issue in the question] **only partially.**"
2) **Interpretation** (3 marks)
   i. Identify one piece of information from the source.
   ii. Start by writing: "**The Source explains / mentions / highlights / shows that ...**" then give details of one point of relevant information explained in the source.
   iii. Write: "**This is important in explaining** [issue in the question] **because it shows / is key to / is an important feature of / means that ...**" then explain why the interpretation is relevant to the issue in the question.

COMPLETE THIS PROCESS TWICE MORE

3) **Wider Contextual Development** (7 marks)

Give more information about an interpretation point, or show how information is missing completely.

   i. Develop information from the source further. Start by writing: "**This source mentions** [detail from source]. **This was ... / This suggests ... / This was because ... / This was when ...**"

   OR

   i. Start by writing: "**However, the Source is limited as it does not fully explain** [issue in the question] **as it does not illustrate ... / it does not mention that ... / it does not show ... / it does not provide information about ...**" then give details that further explain points in the source or provide points that the source does not mention (omissions).

   THEN

   ii. You must then explain why the information you have provided is useful. Write: "**This further explains** [issue in the question] **because it shows / is key to / is an important feature of /means that ...**", then explain why the interpretation is relevant to the historical event / issue.

COMPLETE THIS PROCESS SIX MORE TIMES

Additionally, in place of some of the above points, you could discuss Historical Interpretations.

4) **Historical Interpretations** (2 marks)

Refer to historians and their views which relate specifically to the issue in the question. There are a number of ways you can do this:

- "[Other Author] **believes ... about** [issue in the question]."
- "[Source's View] **is a common opinion on this issue, as** [Other Author] **also agrees, saying that ...**"
- "[Source's View] **is a controversial opinion on this issue, as** [Other Author] **disagrees, and puts forward the view that ...**"
- You don't need to quote here but can paraphrase, or simply explain another historian's opinion on the issue.

GIVE TWO INTERPRETATIONS

 **DON'T FORGET**

If you do not have enough knowledge to provide seven pieces of Wider Contextual Development, you can provide additional Historical Interpretation to gain the marks.

CHECKING YOUR ANSWER

Read over your answer, checking that it makes sense and that no points or sections remain unfinished. Make sure that you have: **1)** provided three points of Interpretation; **2)** provided seven points of Wider Contextual Development; **3)** included two other Historical Interpretations.

 THINGS TO DO AND THINK ABOUT

No matter what issue is asked about in any of the source-handling questions, you will never be asked to provide more than eight pieces of your own knowledge. Assuming that there could be four additional pieces of information in the source, you can ascertain that learning 12 pieces of knowledge on any given issue in your Field of Study is the minimum that you should attempt to remember.

THE QUESTION PAPER, PART 2 – SOURCE-HANDLING QUESTIONS

ALTERNATIVE STRUCTURES FOR THE "HOW FULLY …?" QUESTION

A VARIETY OF APPROACHES

There is no particular way that you are expected to structure your answer: below are some examples of alternative ways that you can do this. Each will allow you to gain full marks. An extended point can gain you four marks in the following way:

- **Interpretation of Source** — Select information from the source and relate it to the issue in the question.
- **Contextual Development (Further Development of interpretation)** — Develop the ideas in the Interpretation further using your own knowledge.
- **Wider Contextual Development (Omissions)** — Give further information that the source doesn't mention.
- **Historical Interpretations** — Provide details of historians' opinions / schools of thought which directly relate to the interpretation.

This structure is simplistic and allows you to deal with each aspect separately, making it easier for you to review the number of marks you have written about for each aspect:

- Interpretation of Source
- Wider Contextual Development (Further Development of Points from Source) (Omissions) (Alternative Historical Interpretations)
- Historical Interpretations

This more complex structure allows you to develop the Interpretations with WCD on a point-by-point basis. This is useful if the source is full of distinct points that can be developed in their own right. If you choose this, there is no need to develop every Interpretation in this way. You can pick and choose:

- 1st Interpretation of Source
- Contextual Development (Further Development of Interpretation)
- 2nd Interpretation of Source
- Contextual Development (Further Development of Interpretation)
- 3rd Interpretation of Source
- Contextual Development (Further Development of Interpretation)
- Wider Contextual Development (Omissions) (Historical Interpretations)
- Historical Interpretations

SAMPLE QUESTION

Source A from *Germany, 1919–45* by Martin Collier and Philip Pedley (2000).

By mid-1923 the party had some 55,000 members, many of whom were attracted by the Nazis' "catch-all" manifesto and the radical nationalism of the movement. Throughout the Ruhr crisis of 1923, Hitler and the Nazi press kept up their barrage against the Weimar Republic. After a failed attempt at direct action on 1 May, the Nazis attempted a further coup on 8/9 November. Known as the Munich Putsch, it was in many ways a farcical failure. On the evening of 8 November, Hitler and some 600 SA soldiers stormed a public meeting in Munich, and Hitler declared that "The national revolution has broken out". The following day [the Nazis] led a march into the centre of Munich only to find their way barred by the police. Sixteen Nazis were killed during a brief street battle in which the Nazis were humiliated. However, Hitler turned defeat into a kind of triumph.

How fully does **Source A** explain the political threat that the extreme right posed to the Weimar Republic, 1919–1923?   12

EXAMPLE ANSWER

The Source describes how the right-wing Nazi Party had some 55,000 members, many of whom were attracted by the Nazis' "catch-all" manifesto and the radical nationalism of the movement. This was a level of support that the Nazis would not receive again until 1927, and shows that they had established themselves as a relatively significant force by 1923. [One mark for Interpretation] The source also describes how the Nazis put pressure on the Weimar Republic by using the media to criticise the government during the Ruhr crisis in 1923. This shows that the extreme right would use national crises to undermine the Weimar government in the eyes of the public. [One mark for Interpretation] Additionally, the source gives details of what occurred during the Munich Putsch, whereby the Nazis and the SA forcibly took over a public meeting in Munich, marched into Munich the next day and were defeated by government forces, ending in humiliation for the Nazis. This highlights the threat posed by the extreme right, as they were willing to use violent methods to achieve their aims. [One mark for Interpretation]

However, the source does not fully explain the motivation that lay behind the Munich Putsch. The Nazis and the SA aimed to lead an armed insurrection against the government in Berlin, starting in the Bavarian capital. They had been part of a conspiracy that included members of the Bavarian government and the Reichswehr. However, the other conspirators had decided not to go ahead at the last minute, abandoning the Nazis. This shows that the threat from the right was quite a serious one, which had occasional support from the army and leading politicians. [Two marks for WCD]

Moreover, the source does not mention that the extreme right had posed a threat to the Weimar Republic prior to 1923. Nationalists reacted badly to the terms of the Treaty of Versailles. This, combined with the shock of the signing of the armistice in November 1918, led to extremist groups claiming that the German people and army had been 'stabbed in the back'. This shows that the extreme right posed a threat, as this rhetoric was used by Hitler to gain support for the Nazis before coming to power. [One mark for WCD]

Additionally, the source omits that right-wing groups were responsible for a considerable number of political assassinations of key supporters of the Republic. The Organisation Consul assassinated Walter Rathenau, the Foreign Minister, in 1922. This shows that the extreme right were able to deprive the Weimar government of some key figures and supporters. [One mark for WCD] This threat can be further illustrated by the assassination of Matthias Erzberger by right-wing forces. He had been one of the politicians who had signed the armistice. [One mark for WCD] Also not mentioned was the assassination of politicians on the extreme left. The leader of the USPD, Gareis, had been killed in Munich in 1921. This shows the level of violence that existed and illustrates how the methods of the extreme right undermined democracy in the early 1920s. [One mark for WCD]

Further, the source does not mention that in 1920, Kapp and General Luttwitz led an attempt to seize power by marching on Berlin with 20,000 troops. The government was forced out of the city, due to the fact that the army refused to support it against other soldiers. This shows that there was a threat from the extreme right, as it was able to bring into question the Weimar government's grip on power, even though Kapp only held power for four days. [One mark for WCD]

Layton acknowledges the threat to the Weimar Republic that the Kapp Putsch revealed: that the army was unwilling to support the government against other para-military groups. [One mark for Historical Interpretations] Meanwhile, Carr believes that the army with its authoritarian views posed a significant threat to both democracy and the Weimar government, that was not challenged effectively. [One mark for Historical Interpretations]

 THINGS TO DO AND THINK ABOUT

You should make the effort to attempt as many sample or past exam papers as you can, to practise using these alternative answer structures.

THE QUESTION PAPER, PART 2 – SOURCE-HANDLING QUESTIONS

THE "INTERPRETATION OF TWO SOURCES" QUESTION AND HOW TO ANSWER IT

THE TWO SOURCES QUESTION

There will also be one question, of this type, to answer in your chosen Field. This question is worth 16 marks. The focus of this question is to determine the view of each of the sources, by using separate points of Interpretation. You should then place the source within its historical context to illustrate how much both sources reveal about the issue raised in the question. Additionally, there are again marks available for providing valid Historical Interpretations. Thus, three components of source-handling questions can be discussed for this answer:

- Interpretation
- Contextual and Wider Contextual Development
- Historical Interpretations

DON'T FORGET

You have approximately 30 minutes to complete this question.

ONLINE

Visit the SQA Understanding Standards website for Advanced Higher History for annotated examples of "Interpretation of Two Sources" question answers. You can find links on our Digital Zone - www.brightredbooks.net/subjects

ALLOCATION OF MARKS

The 16 marks available for this question will be awarded as follows:

Interpretation	6 marks (Maximum of 3 marks per source)
Contextual and Wider Contextual Development	8 marks (which can include details of relevant Historical Interpretations)
Historical Interpretations	2 marks

ANSWERING THE QUESTION

This Question Type will always begin with: "How much do … reveal about differing interpretations of …?"

Although this question seems vastly different to the other source-handling questions, this is similar to the "How fully …?" question in this Paper; the only difference is that there are two sources. It builds on skills developed for the Differing Interpretations question in the Scottish History section of the Higher History Question Paper.

Interpretation

You do not compare the sources directly; you will gain no marks for doing so. Instead, you need to select Interpretation points from one source to establish its view of the issue in the question, then do the same with the other source. Hence, two separate views on the issue should be established. As is normal, content which you select from the source must be explained in terms of how it relates to the issue.

DON'T FORGET

The sources are not intended to contain points that are directly comparable, and the opinions expressed in each may not necessarily contrast. However, each one will outline an opinion on the issue raised in the question. It is these opinions that should be explained and then fleshed out with Wider Contextual Development.

Contextual Development and Wider Contextual Development

There are several ways to gain marks in this section. You could:
- provide more development of Interpretation points selected from the sources.
- provide factual content that the sources fail to mention.

(For each of the methods above, you need to explain why this information is important to the issue.)

- provide more Historical Interpretations or views of prominent historians.

DON'T FORGET

Historical Interpretations can agree or disagree with or provide opinion that is unrelated to, the opinions of either Source. Remember though, when giving details of historians' opinions, they must be explicitly linked to the issue raised in the question.

WRITING YOUR ANSWER TO THE "INTERPRETATION OF TWO SOURCES" QUESTION

Identify the keywords in the question, i.e. the issue that the question is asking you about. Highlight these. It is good practice to briefly plan out your answer before you read the source, by noting down key features of the issue in the question. You should also take the time to think of the various Interpretations of the issue in the question, as this is very much the focus of your answer.

The Question Paper, Part 2 – Source-Handling Questions: Question Types ...

READING THE SOURCE

- Make sure that you read the correct sources.
- Read the information above the source which may give you an indication of why it was produced.
- Read over both sources once, without stopping, to familiarise yourself with the content.
- Re-read the first source for understanding. It may be useful to re-read the first source twice, thinking about firstly what opinion it holds on the issue as a whole; then looking for specific points that illustrate this opinion. Do the same with the second source.
- Now highlight or underline the phrases, sentences or paragraphs in each source that relate to the issue in the question.

WRITING FRAME

Below is a sample structure that you could use.

1) Start by writing: "**The sources provide varying perspectives on** [issue in the question]."
2) **Interpretation of 1st Source** (6 marks)
   i. Start by writing: "**Source [...]'s overall view on [issue in the question] is**"

   ii. Then write: "**The Source explains / mentions / highlights / shows that ...**" then give details of one point of relevant information explained in the source.

   iii. Write: "**This is important in explaining [issue in the question] because it shows / is key to / is an important feature of / means that ...**", then explain why the interpretation is relevant to the issue in the question.

COMPLETE THIS PROCESS FOR EACH INTERPRETATION

3) **Contextual Development and Wider Contextual Development** (8 marks)
   i. Give more information about an interpretation point. Start by writing: "**This interpretation can be further explained by** [provide own knowledge]".

OR
   i. Show how alternative interpretations are missing completely. Start by writing: "**However, the Source is limited as it does not fully detail** [alternative interpretation / historians' viewpoint of the issue in the question]". "**This was ...**", then give details of the different viewpoint and provide further knowledge to support it.

THEN
   ii. You must then explain why the information you have provided is relevant to the issue in the question.

COMPLETE THIS PROCESS UNTIL YOU HAVE EIGHT PIECES OF DETAIL NOT PROVIDED IN THE SOURCES

4) **Historical Interpretations** (2 marks)
   Refer to historians and their views which relate specifically to the issue in the question. There are a number of ways you can do this:
- "[Other Author] **believes ... about** [Issue in the question]."
- "[Source's View] **is a common opinion on this issue, as** [Other Author] **also agrees, saying that ...**"
- "[Source's View] **is a controversial opinion on this issue, as** [Other Author] **disagrees and puts forward the view that ...**"

GIVE TWO INTERPRETATIONS

CHECKING YOUR ANSWER

Read over your answer, checking that it makes sense and that no points or sections remain unfinished. Make sure that you have:

1) provided six points of Interpretation (three from each source), each with explanations of why they are useful in revealing the issue.
2) provided eight points of Wider Contextual Development, in the form of information omitted by the source or Historical Interpretations, and you have explained why each of these is relevant to the issue.
3) include two other Historical Interpretations for full marks.

DON'T FORGET

Remember that this is only one way that your answer may be structured.

 THINGS TO DO AND THINK ABOUT

When answering this type of question, realising the overall view of the source is just as important as identifying individual interpretations. Does it champion one cause over another leading to an event, or place one impact of an event above the rest?

39

THE QUESTION PAPER, PART 2 – SOURCE-HANDLING QUESTIONS

ALTERNATIVE STRUCTURES FOR THE "INTERPRETATION OF TWO SOURCES" QUESTION

A VARIETY OF APPROACHES

There is no particular way that you are expected to structure your answer: below are some examples of alternative ways that you can do this. Each will allow you to gain full marks. Making an extended point can gain you four marks in the following way:

Interpretation of Source	Select information from the source and relate it to the issue of the question.
Contextual Development (Further Development of interpretation)	Develop the ideas in the Interpretation further using your own knowledge.
Wider Contextual Development (Omissions)	Give further information that the source doesn't mention.
Historical Interpretations	Provide details of historians' opinions / schools of thought which directly relate to the interpretation.

This structure allows you to further develop each source separately and could be used if the sources provide widely different views which could be discussed in isolation:

- Interpretation of 1st Source
- Contextual Development (Further Development of Points from Source)
- Interpretation of 1st Source
- Contextual Development (Further Development of Points from Source)
- Wider Contextual Development (Omissions) (Alternative Historical Interpretations)
- Historical Interpretations

This more complex structure allows you to develop the Interpretations with WCD on a point-by-point basis. This is useful if the sources are full of distinct points that can be developed in their own right. If you choose this, there is no need to develop every Interpretation in this way.

- 1st Interpretation of Source 1
- Contextual Development (Further Development of Interpretation)
- 2nd Interpretation of Source 1
- Contextual Development (Further Development of Interpretation)
- 3rd Interpretation of Source 1
- Contextual Development (Further Development of Interpretation)

As above, for Source 2

- Wider Contextual Development (Omissions) (Alternative Historical Interpretations)
- Historical Interpretations

SAMPLE QUESTION

Source A from *History of the Roman Empire, III,14* by Herodian (c. 240).

Severus was becoming disturbed by the lifestyle of his sons and their enthusiasm for public spectacles, when the governor of Britain sent word to him that the barbarians were in revolt and that they were overrunning the country, looting it and causing widespread havoc. He therefore requested additional forces to protect the place or a visitation by the Emperor. Severus was pleased to hear this, for besides being a natural lover of glory, he wanted to raise some victory-trophies at the expense of the Britons to add to the victories and titles won in the east and north. Then again, he wanted to get his sons away from Rome so that they might come to their senses amidst the disciplined life of the army, once they were away from the luxury and high life of Rome. And so, although he was now well advanced in years and crippled with arthritis, Severus announced his expedition to Britain.

Source B from *The Romans Who Shaped Britain* by Sam Moorhead and David Stuttard (2012).

Antoninus Pius was a man with a reputation for shunning warfare unless absolutely necessary. Yet, with an army to keep occupied and generals to placate, it was occasionally politic even for a man of peace to engineer necessities for war. After all, there would be those in Rome who remembered all too well men like the British governor Trebellius whose inaction had prompted his troops to mutiny.

Lollius Urbicus arrived in Britain ... to push back the northern boundaries once more beyond Hadrian's Wall ... It may be that the Emperor saw the need to keep the British troops engaged – there were so many of them, after all. Or he wished to prove his military worth – what better theatre for a spectacular campaign than Britain's frontier, with its notoriously fierce tribes? It was a theatre, moreover, sufficiently far from Rome that news of his legions'

contd

victories could be embellished in their telling. Indeed, at the campaign's conclusion some three years later, Antoninus Pius was hailed imperator, an event he marked at Rome with victory coins.

How much do **Sources A** and **B** reveal about differing interpretations of the reasons why the Romans invaded Northern Britain?

16

EXAMPLE ANSWER

Source A proposes that the Romans invaded Northern Britain to deal with unrest within the empire and to gain military glory.

The source explains that "the governor of Britain sent word to him that the barbarians were in revolt and that they were overrunning the country, looting it and causing widespread havoc". The governor asked Severus to either come to Britain himself or at least send additional troops. This suggests that Severus led an invasion force into Northern Britain in order to subdue unruly natives. [One mark for Interpretation] The view that Roman invasions into Northern Britain were launched to subdue the natives is supported by Guy de la Bedoyere, who states that Antoninus Pius faced trouble in Britain at the start of his reign. [One mark for Historical Interpretations] The source also shows that Severus wanted to put an end to the controversy and tension in the capital caused by his sons, as it states that he was "disturbed by their lifestyle" and "enthusiasm for public spectacles". He thought that giving them military experience would make them mature and hardened, increasing their respect among the ruling class. [One mark for Interpretation] Source A also describes how Severus was happy to be asked because he welcomed the chance to gain military glory, implying that some Roman invasions were motivated by personal impulses. [One mark for Interpretation] However, the source does not fully explain how military glory had motivated emperors. According to Tacitus, the emperor had given instructions to seek out glory by advancing north into unconquered territories. [One mark for WCD] Moreover, the source fails to mention that the pursuit of military glory was built into the Roman psyche and hence Roman emperors and generals would always want to push the frontier forward. This can be seen in Caesar's invasion of southern Britain in 55–54 BC. Correspondence between one of his legionary commanders and Cicero in Rome reveals the excitement with which news of Caesar's invasion was received [Two mark for WCD]. This interpretation of the Roman mindset is put forward by Kamm, who suggests that expansion of the empire would not cease, such was their obsession with war and conquest. [One mark for Historical Interpretations]

On the other hand, Source B suggests that the Romans invaded to ensure the Emperor furthered his reputation.

The source points to problems that previous rulers had with controlling unruly and unoccupied legions and how a previous British governor, Trebellius, had suffered mutiny. It explains that Antoninus was peaceful, but "it was occasionally politic even for a man of peace to engineer necessities for war." This supports the view that Northern Britain was invaded by the Romans in order to allow Antoninus Pius to tighten his control over the army and strengthen his position as emperor. [One mark for Interpretation] Furthermore, the source details how the Emperor used war in Britain to prove his military worth, as it was a place with a reputation for fierce warriors and far enough from Rome to manipulate reports of what was achieved. This affirms the possibility that the Romans invaded Northern Britain as a guaranteed way for the new emperor, Antoninus Pius, to tie himself to military success. [One mark for Interpretation] The view is furthered by the source when it describes that "at the campaign's conclusion some three years later, Antoninus Pius was hailed imperator, an event he marked at Rome with victory coins". [One mark for Interpretation] The view that invasion was used as a tool by certain Roman emperors is supported by the historian Bettany Hughes, who suggests that both Claudius and Antoninus Pius used victory in Britain as propaganda to shore up support in Rome and with the legions. [One mark for WCD – provision of more than two Historical Interpretations]

However, the sources do not mention that the Romans may have invaded Northern Britain in an attempt to protect the peaceful province to the south. Once Agricola had subdued the Welsh tribes, most of Southern Britain was at peace. However, the tribes from the Brigantes northwards were a threat to this peace. Hence, Agricola launched his invasion of what is now Scotland in AD 79 partly in order to secure the gains made in the south. [One mark for WCD] This view, that the aim of invasion was to protect lands already under control, may go some way to explaining why, after a series of roads and forts were built along the Gask Ridge and the Forth-Clyde line, the Romans did not launch another major campaign into the north until the time of Antoninus Pius in AD 139. [One mark for WCD] David Breeze states that they were willing to "interfere in the affairs of adjacent states if they perceived their own interests to be threatened", showing that invasion was intended to protect the empire. [One mark for WCD – provision of more than two Historical Interpretations] This could explain the anger that Severus felt after his first campaign into Northern Britain, that led him to order a genocide against the Caledones and Maeatae. He had made peace with the northern tribes, only for them to have broken the agreement and renewed hostilities. [One mark for WCD]

THE DISSERTATION

INTRODUCTION TO THE DISSERTATION

INDEPENDENT COURSEWORK

The dissertation, also referred to as the Added Value Unit or AVU, is a piece of coursework which you plan, research and write independently of work completed for the exam. It could be thought of as a large essay, although there are additional criteria that need to be met.

Schools differ on when the dissertation is due. However, it will be collected by the SQA in April. This does not mean that you can ignore it until later in the year though. You are expected to read widely from a number of authors and sources and to present your findings in a coherent manner. You will also need a depth of knowledge about your dissertation title. Hence, this will take considerable time.

There are several essential requirements to bear in mind when planning and writing your dissertation.

WEIGHTING AND SUBMISSION

The dissertation is worth 50 marks out of 140 marks: this is over one third of your grade, hence it is important that you make a start on this as soon as possible. The dissertation does not have to be written under timed conditions: it is handed to your teacher once you have planned, researched and written it. It should be typed, and it is recommended that you include a title page, contents page, separate chapters and a bibliography. Reference to historical works in your dissertation should also be acknowledged using a recognised referencing system.

WORD LIMITS

There is a limit of 4,000 words. However, there is a 10% allowance, so between 3,600 and 4,400 words will be accepted without penalty. Exceeding this limit will result in penalties being applied. A dissertation which falls short of 3,600 words will struggle to pass.

This word limit does not include any title pages, contents pages, references, bibliographies or appendices. However, it is important not to include lengthy footnotes or appendices, as this will detract from the flow of the dissertation. Do not use footnotes or appendices to attempt to avoid the word limit, as this may be penalised.

BASIC REQUIREMENTS

In order to pass (achieve more than 24 out of 50 marks), there are several requirements that must be met:

1) **Primary Source**

Your dissertation must have reference to at least one primary source in order to pass. This can be quoted, referred to or described. It may be that the primary source is not a

contd

written source; and description of primary sources such as artefacts, treaties or artwork is acceptable. However, it is important that the primary source is relevant to the dissertation and is used in a way that helps put forward the argument in analysis or evaluation. It is worth bearing in mind that although only one is required, a range of primary sources will help improve your dissertation.

2) <u>Historians' Views</u>

It must also have reference to historians and their views, or schools of thought. Again, although only one is required to pass, a wide range of views and evidence of reading will increase the quality of your dissertation.

3) <u>Referenced Research</u>

You must clearly reference at least one source, using a recognised referencing system. You should use footnotes and a bibliography to show you have undertaken research.

CHOOSING A QUESTION

For each Advanced Higher Field of Study, there is an SQA Approved List of Dissertations, found on the SQA website, which covers the full range of issues within those fields. You need to choose a title that falls within the Field of Study that you are studying. It is recommended that you choose a dissertation question that the SQA has approved.

If you want to make any changes to the question, or you want to choose an alternative title, it is essential that this is cleared with the SQA by your school before you start. There is official documentation that needs to be filled in, namely the Project-Dissertation Title Feedback Form, found on the SQA website.

Please note that the SQA updates and makes changes to the Approved List. Make sure you are working from the most recent version, published yearly, which is available on the SQA website. You should be working from the list published in the year that you **started** your course. If you begin your dissertation before the summer break, it is important you check that your question has not changed due to an updated list being published in the summer months.

PLAGIARISM

Plagiarism can be defined as copying the work of others. It is also defined as taking **ideas** from books, articles or websites without acknowledging it through referencing. If you do so, it will be noticed and may be penalised. Significantly, you may have selected the same, or a similar dissertation title to other pupils, in the school or otherwise. Copying from other pupils, or producing work similar to them, is also regarded as plagiarism.

 ## THINGS TO DO AND THINK ABOUT

When considering the approved list to choose your dissertation title, it may be a good idea to think of what your strengths were when answering Higher History essay question types.

Did you prefer an isolated-factor question where you considered different factors, before making a decision on what one was more influential in a given issue? Alternatively, did you like questions that focused on a concept that you could prove or disprove? Both types of title are available to you in the Approved List.

 **DON'T FORGET**

Make sure that your dissertation title is on the approved list, or that it is approved by the SQA before starting your research.

 **DON'T FORGET**

Academic authors and primary sources will often show bias towards certain issues. Be aware of this when you are reading, and question information which sounds one-sided or inaccurate. It is best to corroborate information from three independent sources. On the other hand, do remember that varying opinions from historians are invaluable to help you construct and support your argument.

 ONLINE

Google Scholar is a useful tool to find books. Use this like a search engine, and it will provide you with a list of books and articles which include references to your search. Be careful of taking information or quotes from non-academic websites – ask yourself if you really want the marker to see references to websites such as brainyquote.com in your dissertation. Links can be found at our Digital Zone - www.brightredbooks.net/subjects

THE DISSERTATION
PLANNING YOUR DISSERTATION

IDENTIFYING KEYWORDS FOR YOUR DISSERTATION TITLE

It is essential that, before you begin reading or any other research, you have a clear idea of what information you are looking for. If you do not, you will be tempted to take notes on everything you read. You will by now have selected a Dissertation Title, and you need to determine the most important parts of the question. Important features to note down include the **main issue** raised in the Title, any **isolated factors** that are identified, any **dates** that are stated, and other words that you think may be significant. These features are the Keywords you will use in order to determine whether texts are relevant to your research, and to help you organise your notes.

It is also important to determine a rough idea of the individual chapters / sections that your dissertation will contain before you begin your research. This will give you additional Keywords to search for and refine the note-taking process. It is possible that you will have already covered the issues surrounding your Dissertation Title in class. If this is the case, the work you have already completed, including class notes, essays and source-handling practice, will be your starting point. However, an alternative starting point is the SQA Marking Instructions which can be found online for past exam questions. Although you will not find essay questions that are the same as your Dissertation Title, it is likely that there will be similar ones.

Example:
Imagine that you have chosen a Title that asks you the following:
To what extent were the weaknesses of the Whites the main reason why the Reds were victorious during the Civil War, 1917–21?
There is an Isolated Factor and dates in this question, along with the main Historical Issue, as illustrated below:
To what extent were the relative weaknesses of the Whites the main reason why the Reds were victorious during the Civil War, 1917–21?
- Historical Issue – "why the Reds were victorious during the Civil War"
- Isolated Factor – "the relative weakness of the Whites"
- Dates – 1917, 1918, 1919, 1920 and 1921

These become your Keywords for carrying out your research and helping you determine if texts are relevant to your Dissertation Title.
If you then consider the SQA Marking Instructions for essay questions relating to the debate over why the Reds were victorious in the Civil War, they are likely to detail numerous factors. These are likely to include "White weaknesses" as a factor, but also list the significance of other factors such as "control of resources", "geographical factors", "the impact of foreign intervention" and "the role of Red and White leaders".
As a result of doing this, you now also have potential chapter headings and/or sub-headings for your dissertation:
- Weakness of the Whites
- Other Factors
    - Geographical Factors and Control of Resources
    - Leadership of the Red Army

RESEARCH QUESTIONS

In addition to the Keywords you have identified, you may want to develop a series of research questions to further focus your research. Additionally, a series of sub-questions could be developed under each research question. Sub-questions deal with specific features of the research question. These can often make it easier to organise your notes.

Example:
To create research questions from the example above, we would take each chapter heading/isolated factor and create a series of questions:
'Weaknesses of the Whites' becomes 'What were the weaknesses of the Whites?'
'The Impact of Foreign Intervention' becomes 'What was the impact of foreign intervention?'

Sub-questions which would follow on from this may be
"Which foreign states intervened in the Civil War?"
"Why did these states intervene?"
"What impact did these states have on the White war effort?"
"What impact did these states have on the Red war effort?"
"What do historians think about the impact of foreign intervention?"
"Did foreign intervention impact any of the other factors I will be discussing?"

ENGAGING WITH HISTORICAL SOURCES AND INTERPRETATIONS

Essential in writing a good dissertation is the ability to engage with, discuss and analyse the views that historians put forward. When you are reading texts written by these and other historians, it is important to recognise their opinions on the issue, as opposed to factual content, and to note these down. To help you do this, it will again be useful to create research questions specifically for this purpose.

Example:
If we consider the above example illustrating the Impact of Foreign Intervention, to create focus questions for Historical Interpretations, you would add in sub-questions such as:
"Which historians support the view that foreign intervention had an impact on the outcome of the Civil War?"
"Do any historians believe that foreign intervention was insignificant?"

TITLES LACKING ISOLATED FACTORS

Although many Dissertation Titles will not have isolated factors, you should prepare Keywords in the same way, as there will still be two, or more, sides to the argument. Consider the question

"Can the Roman invasions of Northern Britain be regarded as successful?"

There is no isolated factor here, but the issue is clear: "the success of the Roman invasions". The question implies that these could be regarded as successful, or alternatively unsuccessful. Meanwhile, there is scope for the possibility of the invasions being partially successful. Hence, the keywords would be:

"Roman Invasions of Northern Britain"
"Successful"

In these types of question, there will usually be a word that allows a measurement to be made – in this case 'successful'. Hence, when deciding on Keywords, we should also add in opposing words, such as 'unsuccessful', or 'failure'.

Research questions for this would then follow:

"What made the invasions successful?"
"What made the invasions unsuccessful?"
"Which historians believe they were successful, and why?"
"Which historians believe they were unsuccessful, and why?"

Sub-questions could be:

"What makes an invasion successful?"
"Was one invasion more successful than the others?"

DON'T FORGET

It is essential that, before you start reading, you identify research questions to give your reading focus, and identify keywords to look for while doing so.

ONLINE

You can find more information on how to identify keywords and on how to create research questions on the Digital Zone – www.brightredbooks.net/subjects

THINGS TO DO AND THINK ABOUT

Before commencing your research, identify the Historical Issue that your dissertation will address. What are the main areas of contention within this issue, and which historians support each side of the argument?

THE DISSERTATION
SELECTING TEXTS AND RESOURCES

A BROAD BASE OF RESEARCH

There is an expectation that you engage with material beyond textbooks and core classroom texts. As well as books, you may decide to use journal articles, web-based resources and a variety of primary sources including newspapers, journals, diaries, photographs, paintings and illustrations. You may also engage with archaeological or social surveys. Meanwhile, it may be appropriate to make reference to artefacts and historical sites.

ONLINE

Education Scotland produced Annotated bibliographies when the Advanced Higher course was first established. You can find these by searching for "LTS Advanced Higher History Annotated Bibliography [*Field of Study*]" or clicking the link at our Digital Zone - www.brightredbooks.net/subjects

DECIDING WHAT TO READ

In deciding what texts to read, it is important to keep your Dissertation Title, Keywords and Research Questions in mind. You could start by asking your teacher, who is likely to have a number of texts that would be useful. There are also Annotated Bibliographies available online for the majority of the Fields of Study. Alternatively, you may want to select the names of prominent historians from relevant questions in past SQA Marking Instructions.

In any case, the first text you read should be relatively short and give you an overall summary of the issue, providing a wide coverage, while not going into too much depth. This will give you an overview of the Historical Issue you have chosen. If you use, or your teacher uses, a core textbook for your Field of Study, it would be useful to take notes from this to begin with.

RESEARCHING FROM BOOKS

When deciding if a book will be useful to you, the best place to start is by considering the chapter headings, paying specific attention to any dates or keywords that relate to your Dissertation Title. If you are looking for more specific information, the index will be of more use, as this is in alphabetical order, lists the main contents of the book and will direct you to specific pages. You may want to start by checking with your teacher, as well as in your school and local libraries for books to borrow. Meanwhile, cheap second-hand copies of books can be found from third-party sellers on Amazon and in second-hand book shops.

RESEARCHING USING THE INTERNET

Online research can be faster and often more accessible. If you have decided to buy books, it is worth checking online first, as many are digitised in part or as a whole. Moreover, digital books can be a great deal cheaper than their physical counterparts. However, there are issues you should be aware of when carrying out research from internet sites. You need to be assured that the websites that you use are reliable. Avoid using sites which can be edited by users, ones which allow you to ask questions and leave comments, and ones where you cannot determine who produced it.

Similarly, be wary of using websites that provide a large variety of quotes from historical figures or historians. If you do use these sites, make sure that you authenticate the quotes first by checking accuracy from another reliable source. If it is a comment from a historian, try to identify the work that it came from. This will help you confirm its

contd

The Dissertation: Selecting Texts and Resources

accuracy, but also reading around the quote in the text will provide you with more information and a deeper understanding of the point.

Primary sources are widely available online, and this is often the easiest place to access these, especially more obscure texts. Images of artefacts and historical sites and buildings can also be found here, and it is perfectly acceptable to include images in your dissertation if it helps illustrate a point or lends weight to your argument.

You may decide to use websites that are unattributed to historians, in order to gain factual information about your chosen Dissertation Title. If you do, it is recommended that you use sites which you know to be reliable. Sites that are linked to educational establishments end with .sch, .ed or .ac and should be trustworthy. Those that end in .gov are official government websites and also should be fairly reliable. Blogs and websites providing answers to questions posed by users are less likely to be fact-checked and hence pose a danger to your research. Therefore, it is essential to be critical. If something does not sound right, question it and check with another source.

Below are some useful techniques to use to receive more accurate search results online:

Search Feature	Less Effective	More Effective
Search by keywords	Why did Stalin carry out purges?	Stalin Purges
Search for words combined in results	Stalin Purges	Stalin AND Purges
Search for keywords within files	Stalin Purges article	*filetype:pdf* Stalin Purges
Search for keywords within websites	BBC Stalin Purges	*site:bbc.co.uk* Stalin Purges
Search for keywords in website types	Stalin Purges educational website	*site: .edu* Stalin Purges
Search for both keywords separately	Stalin Purges	Stalin OR Purges
Prevent common results appearing	Stalin Purges	Purges Stalin NOT Mao
Search for specific phrases	So long as the state exists there is no freedom	"So long as the state exists there is no freedom"
Search for keywords in a title	Stalin Purges Title	*intitle:* Stalin Purges
Ignore the title and search text only	Stalin Purges	*intext:* Stalin Purges
Search for keywords in web address	Stalin Purges	*inurl:* Stalin Purges
Searches where you only know some of the words	Stalin	Stalin *
Search for a definition of a word	Purges	*define:* Purges
Translate a word	What does chistka mean?	Chistka in English

 THINGS TO DO AND THINK ABOUT

Create a list of resources that you want to consult during the research period. You should include respected authors and prominent books in your chosen Field of Study. You should also collate a list of primary sources that you may find helpful.

Make this into a checklist, which can be added to. As you read, you will find that many authors make references to documents, artefacts and other texts. Also, some authors may include advice for further reading. Consider adding some of these to your checklist.

 **DON'T FORGET**

A large amount of the texts you need may be found in libraries. Ask your teachers or school librarian if your school has access to online journals or a link with a university library which you could visit or borrow from. Alternatively, the Mitchell Library in Glasgow and the National Library in Edinburgh have vast collections, including e-resources, and provide free access for pupils.

THE DISSERTATION
DEADLINES AND RECORD-KEEPING

It is important that you keep a detailed record of all planning and research. This will help you to keep track of your research for when you need to locate specific information, and will allow you to reference effectively.

ONLINE

Further advice on the planning and the keeping of records can be found at the end of the Advanced Higher History Course and Unit Support Notes on the SQA Advanced Higher History website. Go to our Digital Zone at www.brightredbooks.net/subjects for links.

SETTING DEADLINES

You should set yourself short- and long-term goals within both the research and the writing phases of your dissertation. It is a good idea to discuss this, as well as the reading you intend to do, with your teacher or tutor. Below is an example of how you may set deadlines:

Example:

<u>Short-term Deadlines</u>

Monday - Read and Take Notes on 'Barrow – Bruce', Chapter 1

Wednesday - Read and Take Notes on 'Barrow – Bruce', Chapter 3

Thursday – Read 'Watson – Scotland', Chapters 2 and 3

Saturday – Search for 'Blind Harry' extracts and the letter to the Hanseatic League online.

<u>Long-term Deadlines</u>

Finish Background Reading – 15th September

Finish Main Reading – 30th October

Draft 1 – 20th December

Draft 2 – 1st February

Final Draft – 15th March

Try to avoid giving vague dates, such as 'Early February', as it will make you more likely to miss your deadline: it is better to be specific and hold yourself to that date.

WHAT TO RECORD

Firstly, write down your Dissertation Title, then highlight and annotate the keywords. Once you have done this, you should create a rough plan of what you expect the structure of your dissertation to look like. This would include your chapter / paragraph headings. Take the time to note down any historians, historical works or primary sources that you think may be useful to you. You should keep this plan prominent in your notes as your research progresses, and make additions and any changes that you find necessary as you go.

You should then make sure that you are recording the information that you gain from your research in a methodical way. This includes factual content, Historical Interpretations and Primary Sources.

When researching from a book or an article, it is necessary to record the following:

- Author – Initials and Surname
- Title of Book / Article
- Publisher
- Date of Publication
- Place of Publication

The Dissertation: Deadlines and Record-keeping

If you are using a digital book, record the same as you would for a physical book, as described above.

If you are using a website, record the following:

- The URL (web address)
- The date on which you visited the site.

If you are reading an article or other type of file online, you should record the following:

- The URL of the site where you accessed / downloaded the file
- The date on which you accessed / downloaded the file.

Example:

Look at the following example of a way you could record the above information:

My Reading and Research Record

Author	Primary or Secondary	Titles OR Name of Website	Publisher, Date of Publication, Place of publication OR URL and date
Fiona Watson	Secondary	Under the Hammer: Edward I and Scotland, 1286–1307	Tuckwell Press, 1998, Edinburgh
	Secondary	National Trust for Scotland	http://www.nts.org.uk/learn/downloads/packs/places/independence-teachers-notes.pdf 1/9/17

You may also decide to keep your quotes, names of authors of Historical Works and their Interpretations, as well as primary sources separate from your main notes. You could create a document like the one below to do this.

My Historiography and Primary Source Record

> **Dissertation Title:** "William Wallace's contribution to the Wars of Independence has been exaggerated." How valid is this view?

Where Sourced (Title, Publisher, Year) OR (URL and Date)	Primary or Secondary	Author	Quote / Opinion
William Wallace, Birlinn, 2012	Secondary	Andrew Fisher	
http://www.sath.org.uk/edscot/www.educationscotland.gov.uk/scotlandshistory/warsofindependence/williamwallace/index.html	Primary	Bower	

DON'T FORGET

When recording historians' opinions and quotes from texts, it is essential that you record the page number of the text that they are found on. This is necessary for referencing and will save you a great deal of time later.

THINGS TO DO AND THINK ABOUT

Decide what method you want to use to record information, and stick to it. Do you want to use a digital platform to do so, or keep paper records? It is important that these are readily accessible wherever you are taking notes, to remind you of keywords and research questions. A cloud storage platform, or a digital organiser that is accessible through your phone, may be best.

THE DISSERTATION
CARRYING OUT READING

APPROACH WITH CAUTION

In your research, you will come across works of varying complexity and may find a number of texts difficult to understand. Many people find reading academic texts challenging, as these are written by academics for other academics, as well as for the public. Hence, they often use complex language and subject-specific terms. More often than not, if you choose to read journal articles, they will be more challenging, while books that can be purchased on the high street will be more reader-friendly.

Many of the texts that you read may be biased for or against a certain viewpoint. Although previously you may have been wary to look out for bias in primary sources, it is important to realise that secondary texts at this level can also show bias. This is because authors are often trying to support their own theories at the expense of others. Hence, be critical when you are reading. On the other hand, biased works can be extremely useful to you, as they can be used as evidence to support or oppose conflicting viewpoints in your dissertation.

EFFECTIVE READING FOR TAKING NOTES

Once you have determined that the text you have selected is likely to be useful, take the following three-step approach to reading, based on research carried out by Keshav (2012):

Step	Rationale:	How to do this:
1: Preview and skim the text	This will give you an indication of whether the text is relevant, and also how long it will take you to read. It will also indicate what sections of your dissertation you will gain notes for. It is at this stage you may decide to divide the text into smaller sections for reading.	Read the chapter / article title and all of the headings and sub-headings. Some articles have abstracts (summaries of the main aims and findings, which are useful to read). Skim over the paragraphs, looking for keywords and ideas presented in the text. Read the first sentence in each paragraph. If reading a chapter of a book, pay closer attention to the first and last few paragraphs, as this is often where authors will introduce and sum up the chapter's contents and their main ideas.

contd

The Dissertation: Carrying out Reading

2: Read the text for Familiarisation	This will provide you with a detailed overview of what the chapter contains and will prepare you for detailed note-taking.	Read the chapter / article / section once through, without stopping. This will be a relatively fast-paced read. Do not labour over sections which are more difficult to understand. It is beneficial if the book is your own or if you can obtain a photocopy of the relevant pages, as it is at this stage that making annotations will be helpful. Highlight or underline relevant sub-headings and keywords. If the text has sections that talk about separate subject-matter, put brackets round the section and write beside the brackets what the focus is. If you cannot make annotations, use sticky page markers, index flags or small Post-Its, which you can then write on in a similar way.
3: Read the text for Understanding	This will allow you to access the detail in the text, providing you with a full understanding of the points being made. It will again prepare you for detailed note-taking.	Re-read the chapter, this time carefully. You will need to slow your pace of reading. Each paragraph usually has a specific focus – try to determine what this is. Look up any words you don't understand. Continue to annotate the text where appropriate. Use different colours of pen / highlighter to indicate different sections within your dissertation. You could perhaps also use an asterisk or other symbols, to point to Historical Interpretations or primary sources.

READING COMPLEX TEXTS AND DIFFICULT LANGUAGE

Try not to be dissuaded if you are finding it difficult to comprehend the information you are reading. There are a number of easy steps you can take to help:

- Ignore sections that you don't understand until you reach Stage 3 of the reading process. If at this stage you are still not understanding large sections, you could ask your teacher for help.
- You can divide chapters and articles into more manageable sections before going through the process above. Treat each section like a new text.
- Carry out an additional reading of the text between Step 1 and Step 2. Avoid the temptation to make any annotations during this reading. Simply reading the text like a novel will help with your understanding.
- Reading out loud can often unlock difficult sections in your mind, as can having a section read to you. You may also decide to use a ruler to read line-by-line to provide extra focus.
- Your difficulty in reading the text may stem from being tired or not being able to focus fully (see the Exam Preparation chapter). Try coming back to the text once you have had a break, or the next day.
- On the other hand, you may decide to delay reading the text and search for a simpler one to read. You can put a complicated text to the end of your reading list and come back to it later. It is likely that the reading you carry out in the meantime will help you when you return.

THINGS TO DO AND THINK ABOUT

It is important to be able to focus fully when reading for research and note-taking.

Try to determine where you read most effectively. Is it at school or in a library? Is it at home, in your room or perhaps outside?

It is also important to discover when you will get the most out of reading. Is it early in the morning or at night; before or after meals?

The environment you read in can also affect how well you read and understand text. Do you concentrate more fully in silence or with light noise in the background? Do you like having people around or being on your own? Does listening to music (with or without lyrics) help you keep focus?

 DON'T FORGET

It is easier to understand the contents of a text if you read over the section fully before you start trying to take notes. If you are finding text difficult to understand, read it once more before trying to take notes. Alternatively, take a break and return to it later.

 ONLINE

If you are reading PDF or Word documents, you can have your PC / Mac read them to you. In Adobe Reader, click the View tab and select Activate Read Out Loud. In Word, you will need to add the Speak command to the Quick Access Toolbar, through the More Commands function. Alternatively use the Immersive Reader function in Word.

51

THE DISSERTATION
TAKING EFFECTIVE NOTES – PART 1

ORGANISING YOUR NOTES

Once you have completed the research phase of your dissertation, you will have a great deal of notes, many of which you will need to reference to avoid any issues over plagiarism. Hence, it is essential that, during your research, you clearly organise your notes.

If you are creating written notes

Keep your notes organised in a folder by using dividers. It is useful for you to know at a glance which author your notes came from, and also what your notes are about. There are two ways that you could think about doing this. One way is to separate your notes by author and title. This will mean that you collate all the notes you have taken from one text together, then separate them from the next text's notes. If you decide to do this, each time you take notes from a book it will be useful for you to use different pen colours to indicate what notes will correspond to what chapter heading in your dissertation.

Alternatively, you could organise your notes by the keywords / research questions / chapter headings of your dissertation. This will take a little more forethought, but will make it easier when you reach the writing stage, as your notes will already be collated by chapter headings of your dissertation. To do this, it is recommended that when reading and taking notes from a text, you have separate pieces of paper for each section of your dissertation. If you select this method, remember to write the author and title of the text before you start taking notes. Then read the text and take notes on the relevant pieces of paper.

Example:

Imagine you had selected the following for your dissertation title:
"To what extent were the roots of the American Civil War to be found in the issue of slavery?"
From this, you may have decided that your chapters will focus on different reasons for the outbreak of the civil war, including Slavery, Economic Considerations and Political Disintegration.
If you are organising your notes by author and title, you would take notes from one text on one continuous set of paper. You would have one colour of pen for information on Slavery, but have different colours for information on Economic Considerations and Political Disintegration.
If using the second method, you would have a separate sheet of paper for each different factor – Slavery; Economic Considerations and Political Disintegration.

contd

The Dissertation: Taking Effective Notes – Part 1

If you are creating digital notes

If typing notes, these still need to be organised. Use the above methods, but you may want to think about organising these into folders on a computer. Alternatively, a more effective method is using an app such as OneNote, where you can create different pages and folders for your notes, and access them anywhere. Just remember to sync your notes after each session so you don't lose any.

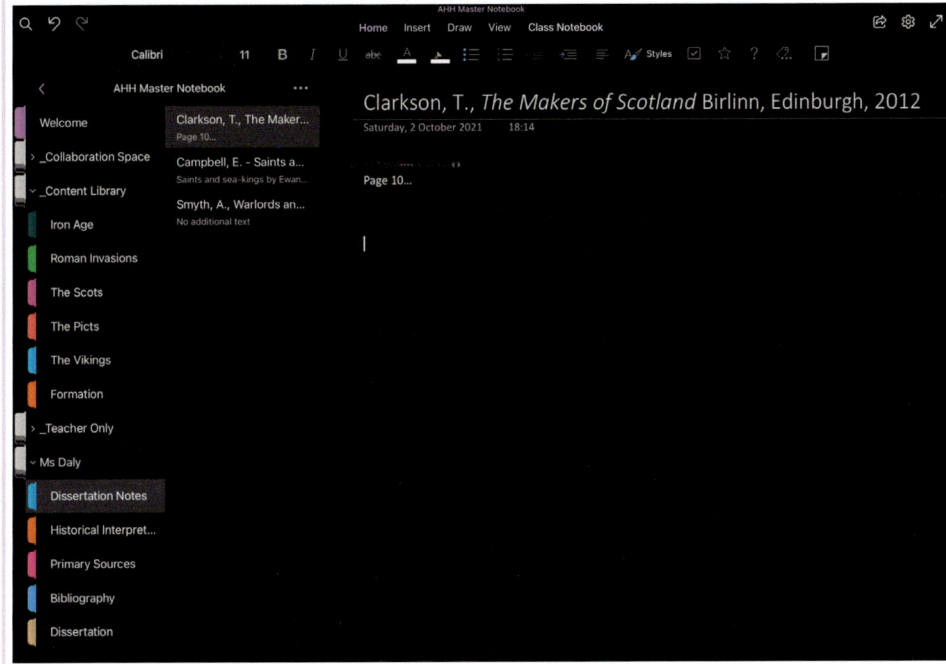

 DON'T FORGET

Remember to record each text and website you take notes on, onto your reading record. This will help you to create an accurate bibliography.

PREPARING TO TAKE NOTES

It is essential that you write down the Author and Title of the text, or the name of the website, you are about to take notes on. Underline this or use different colours, so it can be clearly seen later. If you are taking notes from a certain chapter in a book, it would be a good idea to use the chapter number and title as sub-headings in your notes. If there are headings and sub-headings on a website that you are taking notes from, use these to help divide your notes into clear sections.

 ONLINE

Use an online storage system for notes, such as OneNote, OneDrive or Google Drive, to record your annotations.

 THINGS TO DO AND THINK ABOUT

Decide if written or typed notes would be more beneficial to you. On the one hand, if you are likely to be taking notes in a number of different locations, taking notes digitally on your phone or tablet may be best. However, if you are likely only to have access to a device at certain times, or in specific locations, you may prefer to handwrite your notes.

To collate your notes effectively, use dividers with tabs that you can write on. Go back to your Dissertation plan and research questions / chapter headings. Take a new divider for each one and store them in a folder, separate from your other work.

 DON'T FORGET

If you want to type your notes, you can download Microsoft Office, including Word and OneNote, for free by logging on to your Glow account.

53

THE DISSERTATION
TAKING EFFECTIVE NOTES - PART 2

PRACTICE MAKES PERFECT

If you have little experience in taking notes, it is likely that you will find it difficult to start with. It takes practice to create effective notes – and, to begin with, you will find that you write either too much or too little. It is important to take regular breaks – if you don't, you will lose focus and begin to think everything is worth noting down.

When you are taking notes, have your focus questions at the forefront of your mind. It is often difficult, when reading a text within your Field of Study, not to see everything as relevant. It may help to have these questions in front of you to keep focused.

WHAT INFORMATION TO LOOK FOR

You should be thinking of the structure that you are planning for your dissertation. It should be clear in your head what chapters you are planning to divide your dissertation into. Hence, when taking notes, it may be useful to use different colours of pens / font for each chapter or section. There are three main things to look for when reading secondary texts.

Firstly, factual information to expand your knowledge about your Dissertation Title and to explain aspects of your Dissertation in detail. This will help to add Depth.

Secondly, analysis, historical opinion and argument, to allow you to develop your analysis of key points in your Dissertation. It is important that you record exactly where you obtain this – put the page number(s) beside the quote/information – as this needs to be referenced. This applies to quotations, but also to paraphrased material and to anywhere you mention a historian's name. Analysis and evaluation that is not your own also needs referencing.

Finally, references to primary texts, to other sources and to recommendations for further reading may be useful to record. If one author references the work of another, you should aim to read this as well.

In regard to taking notes from primary texts, it is effective to quote from these if there are stand-out phrases. Alternatively, you may also "name-drop" the author of the source to refer to what they have said. In this case, paraphrase the information, which simply involves recording relevant information in your own words. If you are wanting to refer to artefacts, it is often a good idea to make a brief description of the artefact in your notes.

HOW TO LAY OUT YOUR NOTES

You can reduce time by using abbreviations for words. Depending on your Field of Study, there will be words that recur a great deal, and it is a good idea to develop a shorthand for them, e.g. "government" becomes "govt"; "American Civil War" becomes "ACW". You may also decide to use symbols for certain words, such as '∴' for 'therefore'.

You may prefer to create diagrams, such as flow charts or spider diagrams, instead of using continuous prose. If you are recording a sequence of events, you may decide to create a timeline.

> **DON'T FORGET**
>
> Reference to at least one primary source is essential to achieve more than 24/50 for your dissertation. There is the expectation that you use primary sources to lend to your analysis and support your argument, rather than just mentioning them as an isolated piece of knowledge.

contd

The Dissertation: Taking Effective Notes - Part 2

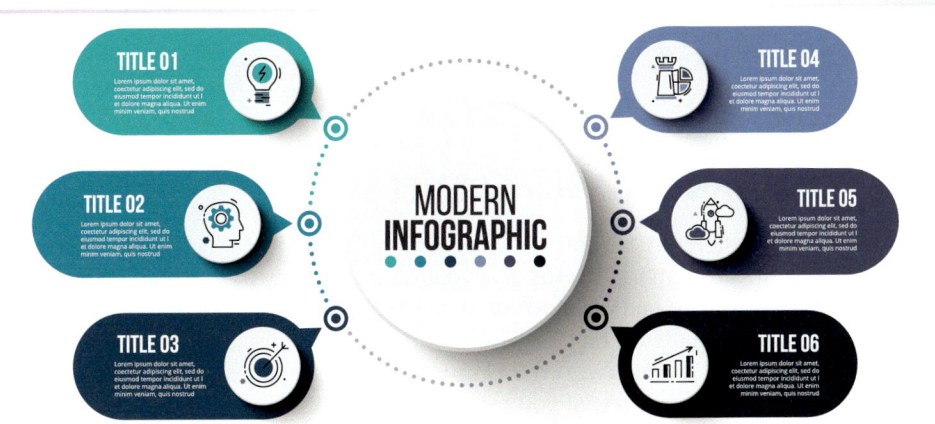

Do not directly copy from the text unless you intend to use the section as a quotation in your Dissertation. Instead, put information into your own words. Try to encapsulate ideas in the text and translate them into language that is meaningful and easy to understand for you. Doing this will help you to understand the information more effectively. Sometimes an easy way to do this is to read a paragraph, and then write down anything you think is relevant without looking back at the text.

Make sure that anything you write down word-for-word is put in quotation marks. You may want to highlight or underline these, or use a different coloured pen to make your quotes stand out. You should aim to take quotes from statements that are key to the arguments made in your dissertation.

DEVELOPING YOUR NOTES

Annotate specific parts of your notes with comments linked with arrows, in order to develop specific ideas. Use different coloured highlighters and pens to accentuate different aspects of your notes. For instance, you may want to highlight the following separately:

- Historians' opinions
- General details and knowledge
- Primary sources
- Background information

If you are going to do this, create a key, note it down on your Dissertation Plan and stick to it. It is important to be consistent, as carrying out your research will be a long process, and when you come to the writing phase you will not necessarily remember what you were thinking at the start of the research phase.

At the end of the note-taking process, write a few lines in your own words to summarise the most significant points made in the text. This will help remind you what is useful about the notes at a later date.

THINGS TO DO AND THINK ABOUT

It is important for your notes to be set out clearly. An effective way of doing this is to divide your page into three columns, with the following headings: Knowledge and Analysis, Historical Interpretations and Quotes, and Thoughts.

1. Use the margin at the side of your paper to record page numbers in case you want to paraphrase, quote or re-check information at a later date.
2. Knowledge and Analysis – a section for general notes from the text you are reading.
3. Historical Interpretations and Quotes – a section for recording historians' opinions. It is essential that you write the corresponding page numbers in the margin.
4. Thoughts – a section for any thoughts you have about what you are reading. Write down where this information would be effective in your dissertation, and make links with other authors you have already read.

DON'T FORGET

When recording quotations, information to paraphrase, opinions and analysis from the text you are researching, make sure you write down the page numbers where these are located. This will save you a great deal of time when you are referencing.

ONLINE

For effective advice on reading, follow the link on the Digital Zone: www.brightredbooks.net/subjects

55

THE DISSERTATION
REFERENCING – PART 1

THE IMPORTANCE OF REFERENCES

It is essential that you reference any work that is not your own but which you decide to include in your dissertation. This will give you the opportunity to show the marker that you have read widely, and will illustrate that you have a knowledge of historians' interpretations and arguments. Engagement with Historical Works is a key expectation of the dissertation and is one of the criteria by which it will be judged. Effective use of a referencing system will also prevent you being accused of plagiarism.

WHAT IS PLAGIARISM?

To plagiarise is to use someone else's work and present it as your own. It is plagiarism if all or some of your dissertation has been produced by someone else, including current pupils or ex-pupils at your own school. You will be accused of plagiarism if you have copied sections from a book, article or website without referencing the body of work. You do not have to directly copy text to plagiarise – taking ideas and putting them in your own words, without referencing, is also plagiarism.

WHAT DO I NEED TO REFERENCE?

It is important to realise that you do not have to reference everything you write in your dissertation. You will be including many commonly known facts that can be found in more than one text or online source. There is no need to reference these.

The following need to be referenced:

- All quotations from secondary and primary sources.
- Where you have paraphrased a secondary or primary source.
- Mention of a historian's name or a secondary source, even if there is no quotation or paraphrasing.
- Reference to primary sources including texts and artefacts, even if there is no paraphrasing or description.
- Reference to specific statistics which are not commonly known.
- Any presentation of ideas, analysis or evaluation that is not your own.

ONLINE

There are a number of online guides that show you how to reference accurately. One of the best is on the University of Western Australia website, and you can find a link for it on our Digital Zone (www.brightredbooks.net/subjects). It provides guides for a variety of referencing systems, giving examples of how to reference different books, journals and websites.

DON'T FORGET

Although footnotes can also be used to further explain or comment on something in the main body of your dissertation, it is not recommended that you do this, as it detracts from the flow of your argument. If footnotes are used too often in this way, they may be included in your word count.

REFERENCING SYSTEMS

There are many referencing systems available for you to use, including those which have citations within the main body of the text, and those which use footnotes. Although the SQA do not have a preference for which one is used, it is important to be consistent – choose one system, and stick with it. When using a referencing system, it is important to be precise in the formatting. Pay particular attention to the placing of full stops, commas and spaces, as well as use of italics. The advice provided on these pages exemplifies the Oxford referencing system.

USING FOOTNOTES

Inserting footnotes

Footnotes are references that are included at the bottom of the page where you have made reference to another work. There is no need to format this yourself, as most word-processors

contd

The Dissertation: Referencing – Part 1

have a Footnote function. On Microsoft Word, for instance, go to the "Insert" tab and select "Footnote". This will automatically insert a number wherever the cursor is located. When a footnote is inserted, the cursor should move to the bottom of the screen to allow you to type in the citation. Do not worry if you subsequently insert footnotes in your dissertation, prior to the location of the first footnote, as the word-processor will re-arrange them automatically.

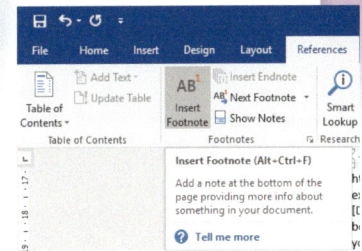

Positioning footnotes

The positioning of footnotes is very much up to you and depends on what you are referencing. If you are referencing a quote, it would be normal to insert a footnote at the end, after the quotation mark. If you are paraphrasing what someone has said, insert it at the end of the sentence(s). If you are mentioning an author or historian by name, but not quoting or paraphrasing, insert the footnote directly after the name. If you are referring to non-textual primary sources including artefacts, insert the footnote after the name of the source, as you would with an author.

THE BIBLIOGRAPHY

A bibliography needs to be included at the end of your dissertation and gives you the opportunity to showcase how widely you have read. Do not be tempted to include reading that you have not used in your dissertation or that you have not read – only include books that were useful to you.

You may decide to have separate sections for Primary and Secondary sources, and indeed a section for websites and other media, in your bibliography. In any case, the titles you have read should be in alphabetical order, by author's surname (see over the page for examples).

FOOTNOTE AND BIBLIOGRAPHY FORMS (OXFORD SYSTEM)

The way that citations are entered into a footnote or bibliography differs depending on the number of authors, if there are editors or translators and if the text is a book, article or website.

In footnotes, it is necessary to include the page number(s) for quotes, paraphrasing and description of an author's ideas. This should be entered as "p. 20", or if you want to show numerous pages, "pp. 20–22".

If your footnote is referencing the same book article or website as the **previous footnote**, you can use the abbreviation "ibid." and simply add the different page number afterwards.

Example:
1 G.W.S. Barrow, *Robert Bruce and the Community of the Realm*, Edinburgh, Edinburgh University Press, 1988, p. 22.
2 *Ibid.*, p. 38.
In this case, *Ibid.* refers again to Barrow's *Robert Bruce and the Community of the Realm*.

If your footnote is referring to the same work by an **author** that you have mentioned in a previous footnote, you can use the "op. cit." reference.

Example:
1 G.W.S. Barrow, *Kingship and Unity*, Edinburgh, Edinburgh University Press, 2015, p. 52. Available from Amazon (accessed 27 January 2022).
2 M. Penman, *Robert the Bruce*, New Haven, Yale University Press, 2014, p. 33.
3 Barrow, *op. cit.*, p. 93.
In this case, *op. cit.* refers to Barrow's *Kingship and Unity*.

THINGS TO DO AND THINK ABOUT

Even if you don't wish to insert your footnotes in drafts of your dissertation, it is imperative you keep a record of every text you have read and every quote you have taken. Choose one way of recording this, and stick to it. It may be an idea to take a picture of each book you read, in order to locate them later. Photos can be inserted into apps such as OneNote.

THE DISSERTATION
REFERENCING – PART 2

EXAMPLES OF FOOTNOTE AND BIBLIOGRAPHY CITATION LAYOUT

Use the table below to accurately reference in your footnotes and bibliography, using the Oxford system:

Type of Source	Example of Footnote	Example of Bibliography Entry
Books		
with One Author	R. Hingley, *Settlement and Sacrifice*, Edinburgh, Birlinn, 2005, p. 22.	Hingley, R., *Settlement and Sacrifice*, Edinburgh, Birlinn, 2005.
with Multiple Authors	O.V. Khlevniuk and N.S. Favorov, *Stalin: New Biography of a Dictator*, New Haven, Yale University Press, 2015, p. 28.	Khlevniuk, O.V. and Favorov, N.S., *Stalin: New Biography of a Dictator*, New Haven, Yale University Press, 2015.
with a Translator	Tacitus, *The Agricola and The Germania*, trans. H. Mattingly, Middlesex, Penguin, 2010, p. 65.	Tacitus, *The Agricola and The Germania*, trans. H. Mattingly, Middlesex, Penguin, 2010.
with an Editor	H. Trevor-Roper (ed.), *The Goebbels Diaries*, London, Book Club Associates, 1978, p. 55.	Trevor-Roper, H. (ed.), *The Goebbels Diaries*, London, Book Club Associates, 1978.
with Editor and Separate Authors	E.W. Mackie, 'The Early Celts in Scotland', in M.J. Green (ed.), *The Celtic World*, London, Routledge, 2005, p. 660.	Mackie, E.W., 'The Early Celts in Scotland', in M.J. Green (ed.), *The Celtic World*, London, Routledge, 2005, pp. 654–670.
Reference Book with No Author	*The Hutchison Dictionary of World History*, Oxford, Helicon, 1998, pp. 45–48.	*The Hutchison Dictionary of World History*, Oxford, Helicon, 1998.
E-Books		
with One Author	R. Evans, *The Third Reich in History and Memory*, London, Little, Brown, 2015, p. 85. Available from Amazon (accessed 24 March 2022).	Evans, R., *The Third Reich in History and Memory*, London, Little, Brown, 2015. Available from Amazon (accessed 24 March 2022).
with Editor and Separate Authors	R. Pipes, 'The Kornilov Affair: A Tragedy of Errors', in T. Brenton (ed.), *Historically Inevitable? Turning Points of the Russian Revolution*, London, Profile Books, 2016, pp. 109–122. Available from Amazon (accessed 29 April 2022).	Pipes, R., 'The Kornilov Affair: A Tragedy of Errors', in T. Brenton (ed.), *Historically Inevitable? Turning Points of the Russian Revolution*, London, Profile Books, 2016, pp. 109–122. Available from Amazon (accessed 29 April 2022).
Articles		
in a Journal	J. Roos, 'Nationalism, Racism and Propaganda in Early Weimar Germany: Contradictions in the Campaign against the "Black Horror on the Rhine", *German History*, Vol. 30, Issue 1, 2012, p. 64.	Roos, J., 'Nationalism, Racism and Propaganda in Early Weimar Germany: Contradictions in the Campaign against the "Black Horror on the Rhine", *German History*, Vol. 30, Issue 1, 2012, pp. 45–74.
from a website	D. Cornell, 'A Kingdom Cleared of Castles: The Role of the Castle in the Campaigns of Robert Bruce', *Scottish Historical Review*, Vol. 87, Issue 2, 2008, http://www.euppublishing.com/toc/shr/87/2 (accessed 12 June 2022).	Cornell, D., 'A Kingdom Cleared of Castles: The Role of the Castle in the Campaigns of Robert Bruce', *Scottish Historical Review*, Vol. 87, Issue 2, 2008, http://www.euppublishing.com/toc/shr/87/2 (accessed 12 June 2022).
Thesis	F. Watson, 'Edward I in Scotland: 1296–1305', PhD Thesis, University of Glasgow, 1991, p. 16.	Watson, F., 'Edward I in Scotland: 1296–1305', PhD Thesis, University of Glasgow, 1991.

DON'T FORGET

Use the same referencing system throughout. The system used in your footnotes should be the same as that used in your bibliography.

contd

The Dissertation: Referencing – Part 2

Websites		
Website	German History in Documents and Images [website], http://germanhistorydocs.ghi-dc.org/ (accessed 25 December 2022).	German History in Documents and Images [website], http://germanhistorydocs.ghi-dc.org/ (accessed 25 December 2022).
Images from a Website	The Lewis Chessmen [online photograph], http://www.nms.ac.uk/lewischessmen.aspx (accessed 20 November 2022).	The Lewis Chessmen [online photograph], http://www.nms.ac.uk/lewischessmen.aspx (accessed 20 November 2022).
Media		
Podcasts	Lenin In Our Time: History [podcast], BBC Radio, 2000. Available from iTunes (accessed 21 February 2022).	Lenin In Our Time: History [podcast], BBC Radio, 2000. Available from iTunes (accessed 21 February 2022).
Documentaries	A History of Scotland: Episode 2 [online video], 2008, https://www.youtube.com/watch?v=A-0e57CU-No (accessed 1 February 2022).	A History of Scotland: Episode 2 [online video], 2008, https://www.youtube.com/watch?v=A-0e57CU-No (accessed 1 February 2022).

 THINGS TO DO AND THINK ABOUT

On one piece of paper or one document, keep a record of all research that you carry out. Make sure that you write down the Author, Title, Place of Publication, Publisher's Name and Date of Publication for every title that you read. Every time you take notes from a website, write down the URL and the date you accessed it.

 **DON'T FORGET**

You need to make sure that you are consistent with your application of the referencing system you have chosen to use. It is normal to have between 20 and 30 footnotes / endnotes overall.

 ONLINE

There are a number of online guides to referencing; most university websites have one. The easiest way to find these is to carry out an internet search for the specific referencing system that you are looking for. The most common ones are Oxford, Harvard, APA, MLA and Chicago.

THE DISSERTATION

THE STRUCTURE AND PRESENTATION OF YOUR DISSERTATION

STRUCTURE

Your dissertation should be structured in the following way:

1) A Title Page
2) A Contents Page
3) An Abstract to introduce the dissertation
4) Separate Chapters (or paragraphs) to address the issue
5) A Conclusion
6) A Bibliography

MARKING CRITERIA

Refer to the Coursework Assessment Task, located in the Coursework dropdown menu of the SQA Advanced Higher History page. In this, you will find the Marking Grid. The grid is divided into four separate categories: Structure; Thoroughness and relevance of information and approach; Analysis, evaluation and line of argument; Historical sources and interpretations.

THE ABSTRACT

An abstract can be thought of as a summary of a piece of work: in this case, your dissertation and its findings. You may want to imagine it as a way for someone who, researching the issue in your question, may decide whether your dissertation would be useful to read.

It should contain several important features:

1. State the historical issue raised in your question, introducing the issue.
2. Provide background to the issue – explain why it is contended by historians.
3. Discuss your research methodology, mentioning prominent (and possibly recently released) primary and secondary sources that helped influence you.
4. Briefly summarise the areas of the issue that the dissertation will address (this could be individual factors or methods of measuring a development).
5. Outline the historical debate – prominent historians who tackle the issue, and schools of thought that have emerged around the issue.
6. State your overall findings and main decision on the issue in the question. This decision should be mirrored in your Conclusion.

There is no separate word limit for the abstract. It is included as part of the overall word limit of 4000 (+/–10%). You may want to dedicate around 500 words of the limit to this section.

ONLINE

The University of Adelaide has a succinct guide to writing abstracts, which can be found using the link on our Digital Zone (www.brightredbooks.net/subjects). It is important to note here that you should combine the criteria for the two types of abstracts described.

FORMATTING

Formatting Feature	Preferred
Font Type	Arial / Times New Roman.
Font Size	12.
Alignment	Justified.
Line Spacing	Either double, or 1.5
Page Numbers	Abstract should be Page 1; Make sure your Contents Page is correctly numbered.
Word Count	On each page; accumulative.
Printing	Single-sided.
Collation	Unstapled – make sure pages are in the correct order.

SETTING OUT QUOTES AND PARAPHRASING

All quotes should be encapsulated in quotation marks. It is up to you if you decide to italicise or embolden quotes. Footnotes should be placed at the end of the sentence where the quote appears, except in the unusual case of having two quotes in one sentence. In this instance, they should be placed directly after each quote. If paraphrasing a source, the footnote should be placed at the end of the sentence where information has been paraphrased.

Shorter quotes

There is a choice when formatting shorter quotes (those that are less than a line in length). It is normal that these are included in your sentence without any special formatting. Alternatively, you can lay these out in the same way as longer quotes.

Example:
> Gildas explains that the Britons were constantly under threat from the Saxon invaders and from the *"foul hordes of the Gaels and Picts"* who descended from the north.

Longer quotes

If your quotes are over a line in length, you should start the quote on a new line and indent the quote. An alternative to indenting is to centre-align the quote.

Example:
> Hindenburg makes it clear that the government were to blame for the loss in the war, insisting that *"Repeated requests for strict discipline and strict laws were never met. Thus, our operations were bound to fail and the collapse had to come: the revolution was only the last straw."*

Providing Provenance and Context

You should also look to provide the reader with an idea of the provenance of the quote. With a secondary text, you should name the historian you are quoting and indicate whether their opinion belongs to a specific school of thought. If quoting a primary source, you should name the source and could, if appropriate to your argument, mention any specific purpose for production or known issues with reliability.

Example:
> In evidence he gave to a government commission investigating the German defeat in 1919, Hindenburg makes it clear that the government were to blame for the loss in the war, insisting that *"Repeated requests for strict discipline and strict laws were never met. Thus, our operations were bound to fail and the collapse had to come: the revolution was only the last straw."* It could be argued that through this prepared statement, Hindenburg was less concerned with answering the commission's questions than with developing the myth of the "stab in the back".

Example:
> According to contemporary evidence, the Picts seem to have been an exceedingly violent group. Gildas explains that the Britons were constantly under threat from the Saxon invaders and from the *"foul hordes of the Gaels and Picts"* who descended from the north. On the other hand, this evidence is tainted by the fact that Gildas, a Briton and a monk, would not have had an impartial view of non-Christian foreigners.

Primary Sources should not simply be included in isolation. They should help advance lines of argument and add weight to decisions made.

 ## THINGS TO DO AND THINK ABOUT

When finalising your dissertation in preparation for submission, you should make sure the pages are numbered. There are functions in most word-processing software to help you with this. It is not normal that a Title Page would be numbered. However, it is up to you whether you start numbering on the Contents Page or with your Abstract Introduction.

 ONLINE

There are a number of online guides that show you how to lay out a piece of writing. One produced by the University of Glasgow is specific for History projects, and you can find a link to it at our Digital Zone – www.brightredbooks.net/subjects.

THE DISSERTATION

THE LAYOUT OF THE TITLE PAGE, CONTENTS PAGE AND BIBLIOGRAPHY

Here is a suggestion of how you may want to set out your Title Page, Contents Page and Bibliography.

THE TITLE PAGE

You should include a Title Page in order to create a good first impression on the marker. This should include your name and the name of your school, as well as your Field of Study and the exact wording of your Dissertation Title. You should also state the number of words included in your Dissertation here.

Example:

Advanced Higher Dissertation

1: Northern Britain from the Iron Age to AD 1034

How fair is it to state that the Viking relationship with Northern Britain was peaceful?

A Person
School A

Word Count: 4,350

DON'T FORGET

Remember to make a final check of the page numbers before you submit the dissertation.

The Dissertation: The Layout of the Title Page, Contents Page and Bibliography

THE CONTENTS PAGE

Including a Contents Page is an effective way of quickly introducing the reader to the structure and line of argument of your dissertation. This organisation should relate to your argument and show clearly the different interpretations that you will discuss.

It should detail chapters and, if appropriate, groupings of chapters. You should number and name the chapters, as well as indicate the page number where the chapter starts.

Example:

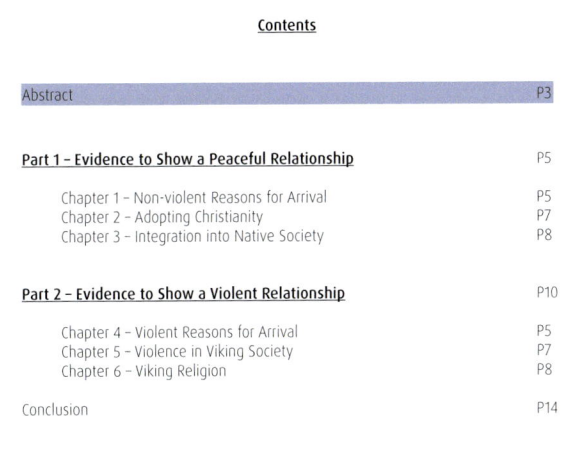

THE BIBLIOGRAPHY

The Bibliography should be divided into separate sections for primary, secondary and media-based sources. Authors should be organised alphabetically by surname. The conventions of the referencing system that you have chosen should be adhered to here.

Example:

Bibliography

Primary Sources

Allott, S., *Alcuin of York*, Sheffield, William Sessions, 1974.

Carruthers B. (ed.), *Anglo-Saxon Chronicle*, Barnsley, Pen & Sword, 2013.

Metz, P., *The Codex Aureus*, Westport, Praeger, 1957.

Secondary Sources

Clarkson, T., *The Makers of Scotland: Picts, Romans, Gaels and Vikings*, Edinburgh, Birlinn Ltd, 2012.

Crawford, B., *Scandinavian Scotland: Scotland in the Early Middle Ages*, UK, Leicester University Press, 1987.

Duncan, A.A.M., *Scotland, The Making of the Kingdom*, Edinburgh, Mercat Press, 1975.

Ferguson, R., *The Hammer and the Cross: A New History of the Vikings*, London, Penguin, 2009.

MacQuarrie, A., *Medieval Scotland: Kingship and Nation*, Stroud, Sutton Publishing, 2004.

Owen, O., *The Sea Road: A Viking Voyage Through Scotland*, Edinburgh, Canongate Books, 1999.

Parker, P., *The Northmen's Fury: A History of the Viking World*, London, Penguin Random House, 2015.

Ritchie, A. & Breeze, D., *Invaders of Scotland*, Edinburgh, Historic Scotland, 2000.

Ritchie, A., *Viking Scotland*, Edinburgh, Historic Scotland, 1998.

Roesdahl, E., *The Vikings*, London, Penguin History, 1998.

Smyth, A., *Warlords and Holy Men*, Edinburgh, Edinburgh University Press, 1989.

Woolf, A., *From Pictland to Alba 789-1070*, Edinburgh, Edinburgh University Press, 2007.

Websites

Works of Simeon of Durham [website], https://archive.org/details/historicalworks00simegoog (accessed 18 November 2022).

 ## THINGS TO DO AND THINK ABOUT

You should create a working Bibliography as soon as you begin reading. Record each historical work or website that you use in order to keep track of your research. Make sure that you record details of the edition that you use so that, if you have to return to it later, you can find it easily.

In this version of your Bibliography, you may want to keep a note of where you sourced the texts from – whether they were borrowed from the school or a library, or they were your own. This will help you locate each one easily for future reference. Make sure you remove these references before submitting it.

 ## ONLINE

There are a number of guides online to help you easily create a Contents Page with the word-processing software that you are using. For Word, click the link on our Digital Zone to use the guide there (www.brightredbooks.net/subjects)

SUMMARIES OF REVISION NOTES

FIELD OF STUDY 1 – NORTHERN BRITAIN FROM THE IRON AGE TO AD 1034

The Key Issues below are the italicised ones from which BOTH essays and source questions can be asked.

IRON AGE / CELTIC SOCIETY

The nature of society

One area of contention among historians is what the main foci of society were. Some believe that religion and warfare were drivers, while others think economic concerns were more influential in shaping the world.

Kamm and **Oram** refer to the warlike nature of society during the Iron Age. **Haywood** also believes the Celts were a warlike people. Meanwhile, **Scullard** points to their skill and training in war. Further, **G. & A. Ritchie** believe that higher social position was gained through excelling in warfare, hence a strong warrior culture existed. They also suggest that settlement types such as brochs and hillforts were defensive in nature.

Alternatively, **Watson** and **Clarkson** do not believe that settlements were built with defence in mind. Moreover, **Cunliffe** suggests that wheelhouses and hillforts could be used as ceremonial gathering points. Further, **Armit** insists that Celtic people were not inherently warlike but were more focused on the economy and religion. He is of the opinion that religion would have been used as way to explain what was happening in their lives and to safeguard the future. This view is also put forward by **Moffat**. Meanwhile, **Cunliffe** also promotes the idea that the world was highly ritualistic, with deposits of precious items occurring throughout the land.

Meanwhile, **Hingley** believes that religion and agriculture were intertwined. He points out that the population was focused on agriculture and metal production in an attempt to gain a surplus, while trade and demonstrating social position were a more important focus than warfare. **Clarkson** also accentuates the extensively cultivated nature of land, showing highly developed agricultural communities, as does **Oliver**.

Demonstrating social status and power

There is also debate over how power was conveyed in society and what aspects helped to determine hierarchy.

Hingley believes that settlement would be used to convey power, such as brochs and crannogs. **Oliver** agrees, citing the building of hillforts by the elites in the south and east, to enforce control. He also sees brochs as a way of conveying power in the north. Moreover, **Turner** believes that evidence from various settlement types in Shetland highlights that they were used to convey social status.

Wormald and **Oliver** suggest that the ability to control the availability of exotic goods and to preside over surplus farm produce would have determined social status.

However, **Kamm** suggests that a warrior elite existed, and those who excelled in battle were held in high esteem, often being celebrated through special treatment at feasts. Meanwhile, **G. & A. Ritchie** agree that metal objects and fortified settlements point to a warrior aristocracy.

On the other hand, **Watson** suggests the abundance of prestige weapons was more about conveying power; and **Cunliffe** agrees that ornate weaponry was used to display social status. In agreement, **Armit** believes that prestige items may have given status, for example the ownership of highly decorated armour and weaponry. Similarly, **Clarkson** believes that power was conveyed through the ownership of high-value items from abroad.

At the same time, both **Armit** and **Clarkson** question the likelihood of uniform practice throughout Northern Britain.

ROMAN MILITARY INVASIONS

Reasons for Roman invasions

There is debate over the reasons why the Romans invaded Northern Britain. Many historians believe that the invasions were down to political circumstances within the Empire. Some think there was the desire to gain military glory and suppress the natives, while others see a desire to Romanise and exploit Northern Britain.

Moorhead & Stuttard explain that the need to display Roman power to those beyond the borders of the Empire was built into the Roman psyche, to dissuade attacks. They cite prolonged rebellion in Northern Britain as a reason for Severus's invasion. This is echoed by **MacQuarrie** and by **Smyth**, who states that tribes in Northern Britain were always troublesome. Meanwhile, **Keppie** believes that the Romans often acted defensively, especially after the Flavian invasion, while both **Breeze** and **Dobson** point to major unrest in the mid-second century that Antoninus had to deal with.

Conversely, although acknowledging there was trouble in the north, **Elliot** suggests that this was welcomed by Severus, who had a great desire for further military glory. Similarly, **Breeze** and **G. & A. Ritchie** point out that the invasion of Scotland in the first century AD would have provided Antoninus Pius with much-needed military accolades. In agreement, **Hanson & Maxwell** believe that military glory was a key factor and that expansion usually occurred around the ascension of a new emperor.

Woolliscroft & Hoffman believe that political motives were the main reason for invasion. Meanwhile, **Breeze**, **Hanson & Maxwell** and **Woolliscroft & Hoffman** point to the fact that the Flavians and Antoninus Pius benefited greatly from the prestige following the campaigns. Further, **Elliot** also cites issues that Severus was having with his sons as a reason for going on campaign.

However, **Breeze** points out that the Romans aimed to dominate and Romanise the known world.

Agricola's role

Although the main contemporary written sources point to Agricola being responsible for the subjugation of Northern Britain in the first century AD, some historians now believe a larger role was played by his predecessors.

Moorhead & Stuttard are of the opinion that Agricola achieved considerable success, leaving Roman Britain more peaceful and prosperous than before. Further, **Breeze** suggests Agricola was effective and successful, citing in particular victory at Mons Graupius. **Kamm** is in agreement, upholding the account given by Tacitus, while **MacQuarrie** suggests that Agricola cannot have been expected to achieve more. Supporting this, **Clarkson** emphasises the logistical barriers overcome by Agricola to establish an effective militarised zone in the north.

Meanwhile, **Southern** points to the fact that there is no firm evidence for other governors being active in Northern Britain, certainly not enough to discount the achievements of Agricola. Further, **Shotter** and **MacQuarrie** attest that military sites north of Brigantian land date to Agricola's governorship, not earlier.

However, **Woolliscroft & Hoffmann** question whether Agricola should receive as much credit, suggesting previous governors achieved more. They believe that Mons Graupius was not the great victory described by Tacitus, but a minor affair. **Hoffmann** also believes that Tacitus is misleading, and much of the work to subjugate the south had been completed previous to Agricola's appointment. **Hanson & Maxwell** agree that much Roman infrastructure below the Tay was already established.

Meanwhile, **Hanson** believes Agricola was an average Roman general appointed for his administrative skills. He believes that Tacitus has greatly exaggerated Agricola's qualities, as does **Woolliscroft**. However, although acknowledging the archaeological debate over the dating of outposts in the north, **Fraser** doubts whether Tacitus would have attributed achievements to Agricola that were not warranted. After all, Frontinus, Agricola's predecessor, was one of Tacitus's potential audiences.

THINGS TO DO AND THINK ABOUT

Try to incorporate historical opinion into your revision notes, being mindful to acknowledge points of disagreement among historians. You should link prominent historians to the main interpretations of each issue in your topic, for use in essay introductions and other areas.

Meanwhile, well-known phrases from established historians, or indeed more traditional academics, may be used in Essay Questions as prompts. It would be helpful if you were able to identify the authorship while discussing that view.

SUMMARIES OF REVISION NOTES

FIELD OF STUDY 1 – NORTHERN BRITAIN FROM THE IRON AGE TO AD 1034

PURPOSE OF THE ROMAN FRONTIERS

There is disagreement over the purposes of the Gask Ridge, Hadrian's Wall and the Antonine Wall. Many historians believe they were built as a symbol of power, while others think that they were intended to mark out the borders of the empire. Meanwhile, some believe they were used as active borders for social and economic control.

Breeze points to the fact that enemies outside the empire needed to be driven back. He believes Hadrian's Wall was intended to separate the Roman world from the barbarian world, helping to reduce attacks. This is supported by **Lynch** and **Clarkson**, and by **Laing**, who sees the Wall as a symbolic end to the empire. Similarly, **Shotter** points to the frontiers established as indications of permanent occupation and dominance.

Although **Hanson & Maxwell** suggest that frontier walls were intended to intimidate those to the north, they were also useful for bolstering an emperor's reputation. **Breeze** also believes emperors often needed to shore up support with impressive advances and structures. **Moorhead & Stuttard** see Hadrian's Wall in this light, while suggesting that the Antonine Wall was constructed to keep troops active as well as to increase the popularity of Pius in Rome, where news of achievements could be embellished. This is supported by **Keppie**.

Meanwhile, **Breeze** thinks that there was a frontier zone which was also utilised for economic gain through taxation, which is supported by **Johnson**, who points to the fact that traders moving large amounts of goods would not have been able to avoid the frontiers. Further, **Maxwell** believes that the Antonine Wall was built to control agricultural land to the south with a strong military barrier. **Hanson & Maxwell** believe the aim was to achieve Romanisation between the walls. Similarly, **Fraser** sees the main purpose of the frontiers being to control and monitor movement. This is supported by **Clarkson**, who also sees it functioning as a method of population control in times of peace. Similarly, **Ritchie & Breeze** see the Antonine Wall as bureaucratic in nature, as does **Oliver**. Meanwhile, **Woolliscroft** is of the opinion that the Gask Ridge was constructed in order to control access in central Scotland. **Breeze** agrees that it would have functioned to regulate movement. **Watson**, on the other hand, sees it functioning to protect lowland Scotland.

Roman methods of control

It appears that the Romans employed various methods to keep the northern tribes subdued, including military might, economic persuasion and the taking of hostages.

Shotter, however, sees violence being used in tandem with bribery. **Breeze** supports this, as does **Kamm**, who believes that the Romans attempted to control the north through negotiation and bribery, citing peace treaties that were agreed with the taking of hostages. This is supported by **Southern**, **Watson** and **Oliver**.

On the other hand, **Moorhead & Stuttard** see the use of military might as a way of controlling the natives. In agreement, **Moffat** suggests the violent crushing of rebellion was commonplace, especially under Severus. He cites the genocide order as evidence of this, as does **Elliot**, who also sees the use of the Classis Britannica as key to Severus's achievements, using the navy for both transport and military manoeuvres.

contd

Meanwhile, **Breeze** also points to the building of military infrastructure, with installations combining frontier walls with signalling towers and forts spread throughout the province and located in "enemy" territory. **Keppie** explains that these were used, abandoned and then re-used when necessary. In agreement, **Elliot** describes how Severus and Caracalla recommissioned much of the military infrastructure around the Forth-Clyde isthmus and the Gask Ridge, while building transport links in an attempt to provide ways to ensure permanent pacification.

Success of the Roman invasions

Another area of contention is whether the invasions were successful or not.

Smyth determines that all three invasions resulted in failure. Further, **Watson** believes Scotland was never really part of the Roman Empire. Meanwhile, **Clarkson** sees opportunities being lost by Agricola in pursuit of the enemy after Mons Graupius.

On the other hand, **Kamm** believes Agricola's account of Flavian glory is accurate, while **Hind** is of the opinion that tribes of Northern Britain were crushed by Agricola. Additionally, **Fields** views the Antonine invasions as providing a buffer between "barbarian" lands and Romano-Britain proper. Further, **Breeze** points to the fact that Severus's invasion resulted in peace throughout the third century AD.

Reasons for Roman failure

There is conjecture over why the Romans failed to conquer the north. Some historians believe there was too much opposition from the natives. Others believe that geographical factors and indigenous social structures played a part. There is also the view that there was a lack of drive to conquer Northern Britain.

Both **Breeze** and **Dobson** think that the Northern British tribes could have been conquered if the will was there, but it was not. This is supported by **Clarkson**, and by **Maxwell**, who believes Britain was on the periphery of Roman concerns. **Elliot** also suggests lack of political will as a reason, stating that certainly after the Flavian conquest, the empire lost interest. Further, **Woolliscroft** sees a lack of economic incentive to conquer Northern Britain. **Breeze** also believes that problems elsewhere in the empire averted focus from Northern Britain. Further, **Clarkson** believes that jealousy of Agricola's achievements on the part of the emperor stopped him achieving more.

Alternatively, **Richmond** takes the view that northern tribes were just too strong. In the same vein, **Oliver** and **MacQuarrie** believe that successive Roman invasions failed to deal with the guerrilla tactics and persistence of the natives.

Meanwhile, **Woolliscroft**, **Mattingly** and **James** believe that lack of social structures prevented the Romans from conquering Northern Britain. **Lynch** tends to agree that the North was politically divided but also accentuates the geographical barriers encountered by the Romans. Conversely, **Oliver** believes that geographical difficulties were just a convenient excuse for failure.

ONLINE

The Roman Gask Project is a long-running archaeological research project led by Dr D. J. Woolliscroft and Dr B. Hoffmann. It details research being carried out on and around the Gask Ridge and provides a number of academic papers on the subject of Roman Scotland. It can be found by clicking the link on our Digital Zone – www.brightredbooks.net/subjects

DON'T FORGET

It is essential to include historiography in each essay in order for that essay to receive more than 12 out of 25 marks.

THINGS TO DO AND THINK ABOUT

Try to incorporate historical opinion into your revision notes, being mindful to acknowledge points of disagreement among historians. You should link prominent historians to the main interpretations of each issue in your topic, for use in essay introductions and other areas.

Meanwhile, well-known phrases from established historians, or indeed more traditional academics, may be used in Essay Questions as prompts. It would be helpful if you were able to identify the authorship while discussing that view.

SUMMARIES OF REVISION NOTES

FIELD OF STUDY 1 – NORTHERN BRITAIN FROM THE IRON AGE TO AD 1034

PICTISH SOCIETY

Pictish origins

There is debate around whether the Picts were a Celtic people. Both **Clarkson** and **Foster** believe they were Celtic like the other peoples living in the region. **Foster** points to the fact that they spoke a form of P-Celtic language similar to the Britons. **MacQuarrie** and **McHardy** also support this view. Meanwhile, **Fraser** says that the notion of a migration from overseas cannot be supported by the evidence. Further, **Watson** believes that racially and culturally, there was essentially no difference between the Celtic tribes of Britain. Moreover, **Carver** is certain that they are not a separate race, and were Celts, like the other Britons on the island. He believes historians have attributed non-Celtic origins to the Picts in order to explain their reputation for having strange customs.

However, **Henderson** believes that they spoke a non-Celtic language, and this explains why they were so distinctive compared to other Celtic peoples in the north. She also indicates that they may have been in Northern Britain before the Celts arrived. **Forbes** also sees possible connections to a non-Celtic language in the distant past.

The distinctiveness of the Picts

One issue debated by historians is why, and to what extent, an understanding of Pictish society remains elusive. Some historians point to their still undeciphered symbol stones, while others cite their origins, language, succession laws and barbarity as setting them apart. Alternatively, other historians believe that they were similar to all other barbarian societies.

The more dated work of **Wainwright** suggests that they were widely different to other barbarian societies.

However, **Clarkson** sees them simply as one of the three Celtic-speaking tribes of Northern Britain. Their perceived distinctiveness only derives from the fact that they have been set apart by their contemporaries, according to **Smyth** and **Ritchie**. In fact, **Foster** is of the opinion that the Picts are seen as different only due to the lack of knowledge we have about them. This is supported by **Oliver**, who believes that their mysteriousness derives from a lack of understanding. Further, **Clarkson** sees their northerly position as setting them apart from the rest. Additionally, **Watson** sees close relations between the Pictish, Celtic and Roman Churches. Moreover, **Smyth** believes that they were a Celtic people and their language reflected this, while **Aitchison**, **Alcock** and **Clarkson** see them as politically, militarily and culturally similar to others.

However, **Henderson**, **Duncan** and **G. & A. Ritchie** believe that they chose their kings by matrilineal succession and hence were different to their neighbours. On the other hand, **Fraser** asserts that belief in Pictish matrilineal succession is naively based on contemporary evidence. **Smyth** and **MacQuarrie** point to the fact that inheritance was not always from father to son.

Meanwhile, **Ritchie** and **Carver** believe they were a warrior society based on old values, as does **Oliver**. **Smith** agrees with this, stating that there was a warrior elite within Pictish society. Alternatively, both **Aitchison** and **Lynch** believe that they were warlike, but this was a common trait among northern British tribes. This is supported by **Watson**, who sees the Picts as comparatively warlike.

The purpose of the symbol stones

Another contentious issue is the purpose of the Pictish symbol stones. Some believe they were memorials and had religious or military significance, while others believe that they indicate political or social organisation.

Thomas views stones with a single animal as boundary markers for division of territory. **Wainwright** and **Henderson** also saw them as tribal boundary markers, while **Samson** views them in terms of sounds of Pictish names. **Clarkson** also sees the symbols as representing personal names.

Meanwhile, **Ritchie** believes that they represent marriage contracts and show lineage. This is supported by **Jackson**, who sees the stones as records of marriage treaties in order to mark out political boundaries and division of land among families.

At the same time, **Thomas** views stones with two and four symbols as memorials. Similarly, **L. & J. Laing** believe that they may have been representations of objects that had been placed in graves in earlier times. Hence the stones became grave-markers for important people. **MacQuarrie** echoes the opinion that they were funerary monuments.

Meanwhile, **Foster** suggests that Class II stones celebrate secular and religious life while demonstrating a growing acceptance of Christianity. She believes that the purposes vary between tribes and over time, but most likely had religious significance. This view is taken further by **Forbes**, who sees an astronomical connection, with the symbols linked to the arrangements of the stars, indicating specific dates.

contd

Summaries of Revision Notes: Field of Study 1 – Northern Britain from the Iron Age to AD 1034

KINGDOM OF THE SCOTS

Origins

There are now historians who challenge the traditional view that the Gaels originated in Ireland, suggesting that they were a group indigenous to the British mainland.

Traditionalists such as **Bannerman** and **Smyth** talk of migration from Ireland spread over a number of centuries, relying on accounts of contemporary writers.

However, while **Foster** agrees that they had cultural connections with Ireland, she sees the suggestion that they were a colony as questionable, there being no archaeological evidence to support this. **Campbell** goes further, believing they were indigenous to the Scottish mainland, citing archaeological and topographical evidence. He challenges the traditional view and sees the Scots as linguistically linked with Ireland, but culturally divergent. He discounts the contemporary sources on Scots origins. This view is supported by **Alcock**, and **Fraser**, and by **Clarkson**, who details numerous instances of linguistic displacement which counter previous attempts to link the origin of the Scots to Ireland. **Aitchison** is in agreement, stating that cultural similarities with Ireland stem from trade.

Societal influences

Traditional historians accentuate cultural influences from Ireland, although modern historians and archaeologists have also made more international connections.

Campbell points to the fact that Scots culture was steeped in religion and Christianity. **G. & A. Ritchie** note close relations between the religious and political spheres. Church officials often acted as advisers for kings and the nobility. They agree with **Foster**, who discusses how the Church and nobility became the king's representatives, mormaers and thanes in local areas, leading to the advent of feudal contracts. This is echoed by **Lynch**, **Foster** and **MacQuarrie**, who see the Church as providing legitimacy to royal succession. **Foster** and **Oliver** also believe that the Church instigated a change in the nature of society, promoting peace and more diplomatic succession practices.

Campbell and **Watson** point to the influence of literature on the Scots, allowing the development of law and administration. **Watson** sees a well-organised kingdom with the beginnings of a sophisticated democracy. Further, **Lynch** sees a highly developed fiscal system which allowed for efficient collection of tribute and arrangement for military service.

Meanwhile, **Campbell** believes that Irish culture influenced the Scots, who were sea-farers in close contact with the Irish, but with their own distinct culture. He cites well-developed trading networks with strong links to Ireland, but also to continental Europe. Dal Riata was multi-cultural and an important hub in north-west Europe. **Watson** sees strong links throughout the Irish Sea and the Mediterranean. Further, **Oliver** also acknowledges the far reach of Scots traders who were in contact with Mediterranean ports.

 ONLINE

Tim Clarkson's blog, Senchus: Notes on Medieval History, can be found by clicking the link on our Digital Zone (www.brightredbooks.net/subjects). Clarkson has written books on the Picts, the kingdom of Strathclyde, the Scots and the Vikings. His blog contains up-to-date information on developments in Scottish early medieval history. He also has a blog dedicated to Vikings: SASVA.

 THINGS TO DO AND THINK ABOUT

In order to help you remember prominent historiography, you may want to create tables similar to the one below.

Issue	List of Factors / Sides of Argument	Supporting historians and main lines of thought
Viking Migration	Acquisition of land	...
	Potential for trade	...

 DON'T FORGET

It is good practice to outline the main interpretations of a historical issue in the introductions of your essays.

69

SUMMARIES OF REVISION NOTES

FIELD OF STUDY 1 – NORTHERN BRITAIN FROM THE IRON AGE TO AD 1034

VIKING INVASIONS AND IMPACT

Why the Vikings arrived

Historians discuss the motivation for the Vikings' arrival in Northern Britain. Some believe that they were forced out of Scandinavia and migrated as a result of a demand for land. Others point to opportunities for raiding and trading.

Parker and **Oliver** point out that reasons for the arrival of the Vikings varied as time progressed.

Ferguson and **Oliver** believe that many Vikings were forced out of Scandinavia due to conflict and the need for land.

Richards, **Smyth** and **Ritchie** also emphasise that Viking raiders were struggling to find available land back home. Moreover, **Winroth** suggests many Vikings were not able to assert their dominance at home. **Jones** also cites the importance of the need for land due to an expanding population in Scandinavia. Further, **Crawford**, **Duncan**, **Roesdahl** and **Smyth** point to the fact that the Vikings felt at home in the Northern and Western Isles, as there was a similar coastal topography and climate.

However, **Smyth** also cites the attraction of wealthy sites to attack and steal from. **Roesdahl** also sees this as the prime motivator, as do **Clarkson** and **Oliver**, especially in the initial phases of arrival. Further, **Muir** and **Walker** are of the opinion that the monastic sites offered easy pickings, resulting in successive raids.

On the other hand, **Woolf** believes that economic considerations were key to their arrival. Similarly, **Crawford** believes that access to new sea roads and the consequent potential for increased trade were key factors. **Roesdahl** also accentuates the strategic value of Northern Britain and especially the Northern Isles. However, she suggests that this was so attractive because increased access to trading routes also gave further opportunity for piracy.

The impact of the Vikings

There is debate over how fully the Vikings overwhelmed different parts of Northern Britain.

Driscoll and **Smyth** believe that they had an enormous impact on society. Further, **Crawford** is of the opinion that Shetland, Orkney and the north-west were annexed by the Vikings. **Owen**, **Richards** and **Duncan** also cite place-name evidence for this takeover, with the Isles becoming wholly Scandinavian. **Roesdahl** is in agreement that in the Northern Isles, where the Vikings assumed total power, there was a violent takeover of native farms. **Owen** also suggests that the disappearance of the Picts here may have been the result of Viking domination. However, **Owen** sees the Vikings as holding less of a grip on power in the Western Isles.

Long-term, **Duncan** believes the threat of the Vikings changed the political and cultural landscape of western Scotland. In support of this, **Watson** attributes political chaos in Dal Riata and Pictland to them. Similarly, **Roesdahl** sees political domination with the establishment of seats of Viking chiefs and earls. Further, **Driscoll** sees the Vikings as responsible for changing the political landscape of Strathclyde and Dal Riata permanently.

A violent people

There is debate over the nature of Viking impact and whether they only brought fear and destruction.

Owen believes that integration would not have occurred peacefully in the Northern Isles, while **Duncan** also sees evidence of violence in settlement here.

However, **Aitchison** points to the fact that it was a violent time and hence the Vikings were acting as others did. Further, **Roesdahl** also believes that the Vikings' destructive influence has been exaggerated, due to writers' nationalistic and religious feeling as well as poetic licence. This is echoed by **Oliver** and by **Owen**, who thinks that they have been painted in a bad light by contemporary writers because of their pagan beliefs.

On the other hand, **Smyth** points to the consistency of reports regarding Viking ferocity and aggression from all across Europe. Further, **Crawford** believes that the contemporary "British" writers were justified in their horror and terror.

However, **Ritchie** also sees evidence of considerable peaceful integration. This view is shared by **Richards** and by **Crawford**, who believes linguistic evidence points to a more peaceful integration in the Western Isles.

contd

Graham-Campbell & Batey believe that Northern people embraced Scandinavian culture, while the Vikings were willing to assimilate peacefully into the Christian world.

Inability to resist the Vikings

There is discussion over why the Vikings were able to operate almost unhindered. Some historians believe that much of Northern Britain was too remote. Others point to the ferocity of the Vikings themselves.

Both **Jones** and **Crawford** point to the fact that much of Northern Britain was too remote and hence vulnerable. Further, **Aitchison** believes that settlement was too sparse to be easily defended and also points to how militarily unprepared Northern British kingdoms were.

Meanwhile, **Roesdahl** attributes the Vikings' success to the mobility of their forces. **Aitchison** stresses the ability of the Vikings to devastate. Further, **Smyth** acknowledges the speed, fury and savagery of Viking methods.

FORMATION OF THE KINGDOM OF ALBA

Reasons for the formation of Alba

There is debate over the factors that led to the unification of Northern Britain. Many believe that pressure from the Vikings was key to forcing unification. Others think long-term factors such as the similarities in culture were important.

Some believe Kenneth MacAlpin had a significant role, such as **Walker**, and **Hume Brown**, and **Duncan**, who sees him as a successful warlord. However, **Smyth** is critical of the plaudits that Kenneth MacAlpin has been given. **Driscoll** regards his role as myth and propaganda. His opinions are supported by **Foster**, who believes that the Treachery of Scone did not occur and that the Picts were not wiped out, but survived after MacAlpin's ascension. In agreement, **Broun** points to the fact there is little evidence for the military achievements of MacAlpin. Meanwhile, **Foster** believes MacAlpin's reputation was down to the fact that successive generations claimed descent from him to strengthen their own claims to power. An alternative explanation is offered by **Duncan**, **Smyth**, **Mackie** and more recently **Driscoll** and **Broun**, who see pressure from the Vikings as key. **Oliver** also cites the Vikings as a highly influential factor. Further, **Watson** sees Pictland descend into administrative chaos after the Viking victory of AD 839. Moreover, **Crawford** and **Owen** cite Viking raids on Dal Riata leading to closer ties with Pictland as the Irish Sea became less appealing. **Crawford** and **Carver** also believe Pictland was severely weakened by them.

Foster thinks that the church was key in unifying the different societies, and that Gaelic culture gradually replaced that of the Picts. Meanwhile, **Crawford**, **Aitchison** and **Walker** agree long-term influences and cultural amalgamation led to unification. Further, **Lynch** sees the increasing Scottishisation of Pictland. This is supported by **Clarkson**, who sees Pictish, and Scots culture merging into one by the early ninth century. Conversely, **Watson** does not see a union between Pictland and Dal Riata but a continuation of the Pictish kingdom under new political conditions.

ONLINE

Websites focusing on more localised archaeology provide transcripts of lectures among other information. The Trimontium Trust focuses on Roman archaeological discoveries made in the Scottish Borders. It has hosted lectures by prominent historians, details of which can be found by clicking the links on our Digital Zone (www.brightredbooks.net/subjects). Further, the Galloway Picts website contains information on the development of society in the south-west of Scotland, including the kingdom of Rheged.

DON'T FORGET

To meet the minimum requirements for historiography in essays, it is acceptable to refer to relevant historians and their opinions more generally. However, to gain Historical Interpretation marks in Source-Handling questions, historiography has to be relevant and it needs to give details of a specific interpretation.

ONLINE

Go to www.brightred.books.net to see a list of academic publications which would be useful for further research.

THINGS TO DO AND THINK ABOUT

The following may be found useful as core textbooks:

Ewan Campbell, *Saints and Sea-Kings: The First Kingdom of the Scots* (Birlinn, 1999)
Martin Carver, *Surviving in Symbols: A Visit to the Pictish Nation* (Birlinn, 1999)
Stephen Driscoll, *Alba: The Gaelic Kingdom of Scotland AD 800–1124* (Birlinn, 2002)
Richard Hingley, *Settlement and Sacrifice: The Later Prehistoric People of Scotland* (Birlinn, 1998)
Gordon Maxwell, *A Gathering of Eagles: Scenes from Roman Scotland* (Birlinn, 2005)
Olwyn Owen, *The Sea Road: A Viking Voyage Through Scotland* (Birlinn, 1999)

SUMMARIES OF REVISION NOTES

FIELD OF STUDY 2 – SCOTLAND: INDEPENDENCE AND KINGSHIP, 1249–1334

The Key Issues below are the italicised ones from which BOTH essays and source questions can be asked.

THE KINGDOM UNDER ALEXANDER III, 1249–1286

The strength of the Crown under Alexander III

There is debate over how united Scotland was during the reign of Alexander III and to what extent a true "Community of the Realm" had developed.

Barrow holds the opinion that Alexander increased royal authority. He also believes that the Scottish economy and the idea of a Scottish community grew during King Alexander III's reign. **Reid** also believes that Alexander III increased the influence of the Scottish crown over the people of Scotland, with the King being more able to exercise his feudal rights by 1286. Similarly, **MacQuarrie** believes Scotland was stable, and Alexander was able to exert his authority with ease. Both **Duncan** and **Nicholson** see a Community of the Realm having developed by the time of Alexander III's death.

On the other hand, **Duncan** held the belief that there were still diverse loyalties among the Scottish nobles that reappeared in times of strife. Similarly, **Lynch** is of the opinion that Alexander III was reliant on the cooperation of the nobility.

Extent of national security on the death of Alexander III

There is conjecture over how secure the kingdom of Scotland was at the end of Alexander III's reign.

Lynch believes that there was too much reliance on the nobles.

However, **MacQuarrie** sees a secure kingdom, as does **Barrow**, who proposes that Alexander was able to inspire loyalty. **Nicholson** and **Duncan** are in agreement. Meanwhile, **M. Brown** suggests that this respect extended as far as the King of England, although he does state that Edward was cautiously staking his claim on the lands of his brother-in-law.

THE GUARDIANSHIP AND THE GREAT CAUSE, 1286–1292

Seriousness of threats to Scotland

There is debate over what posed the most serious threat to Scotland in the immediate aftermath of Alexander III's death. Some believe it was the threat of English overlordship, while others contest that factionalism among the nobles was more serious.

Prestwich believes that the inability of the Scottish nobility to unite was a considerable threat to the security of the Scottish kingdom, while **Nicholson** also accentuates the seriousness of this. Exemplifying this, **Penman** argues that Bruce was acting in defiance of the majority of Scottish nobility. This view is supported by **Young**, who claims that the Comyns represented unity and the true desires of the Community of the Realm. The threat from the Bruces is also highlighted by **McNamee**.

On the other hand, **Barrow** believes that the Bruce faction remained loyal to Scotland and that it was the threat from Edward I and England that was more severe.

Success of the Guardianship in governing the Kingdom

There is debate over how successful the Guardians were in carrying out their responsibilities.

Fisher is of the opinion that the Guardians were unable to effectively govern Scotland. This is supported by **M. Brown**, who refers to their need to involve Edward I in order to keep the peace. Moreover, **Young** believes that there was familial bias within the Guardianship, being disproportionately influenced by the Comyn faction. Meanwhile, **M. Brown** also believes that the Guardianship was ineffectual when trying to unite the squabbling nobility.

Conversely, **Barrow** believes that the Guardians operated effectively and instilled a greater sense of community among the nobility. This is supported by **Morris**, who points out that the Scots' reply to Edward's demands at Norham

contd

Summaries of Revision Notes: Field of Study 2 – Scotland: Independence and Kingship, 1249–1334

was robust. In support of the Guardianship, **Watson** and **MacQuarrie** believe that the marriage proposal within the Treaty of Birgham was a success. **McNamee** also agrees that the Guardians achieved security for Scotland in their early negotiations with Edward. **Lynch** also sees the Guardians managing an evolving situation satisfactorily, while **Oliver** believes they were able to prevent rival factions from tearing the country apart.

On the other hand, **Bingham** is of the opinion that the Guardianship failed in protecting Scotland from the aggression of the English crown.

The nature of King Edward's involvement in the Great Cause

There is debate over Edward's intent during the Great Cause and whether this had an impact on its longevity. Some believe that he was acting in his own interests, while others suggest that there was at least some attempt to carry out his duties ethically.

MacQuarrie believes there was a sinister intent to Edward's approach. He agrees with **Barrow**, who thinks that the King of England intended to erode Scottish independence. **Nicholson** also sees Edward act in his own self-interest towards Scotland prior to the Great Cause. In agreement, **Lynch** is also critical of Edward's tactics during the Great Cause, and of his selfish interpretation of feudal rights. Similarly, **Prestwich** says Edward was acting in his own interests. Meantime, **Barrow** believes he aimed to take control all along, although he does acknowledge that the decision was legally appropriate. Furthermore, **Lynch** suggests that Edward made sure to elongate the process.

Meanwhile, **Powicke** believes Edward acted with good intentions. Further, **Nicholson** points to his long-held belief that he had claim to be overlord of Scotland. **Penman** also supports the idea of Edward acting properly, and that the time taken was justified.

Motivations of the Guardianship and the Scottish nobility

There is debate over what drove the Scottish nobles to act after the death of Alexander III. Some believe that they were driven by selfish motivations, while others suggest an attempt to act in the best interests of crown and country.

Barrow believes that the Guardianship represented a communal attempt to put factionalism aside. This is supported by **Nicholson**, who stresses the attempts of the Guardians to act in the best interests of the kingdom.

However, **Young** is of the opinion that the Comyns had too much of a say, if the Guardianship was to truly keep all factions happy. Meanwhile, **Penman** points to the great divisions and instability caused by the hostile nature of Robert Bruce.

The rightful heir?

There is debate over which of the competitors to the Scottish throne had a stronger claim.

Many historians support the view that Balliol was the rightful heir, including **Barrow**, **Penman** and **Young**. All believe Bruce had a claim but it was weak, as do **Traquair** and **Beam**. **Oliver** also believes Balliol was the correct choice. Furthermore, **Lynch** finds it telling that Bruce did not even have the full support of his own chosen representatives at the judgement.

However, **Prestwich** points to deep divides among the nobility which led to the succession crisis. **Bingham** points out that the Bruce claim was valid, but that Bruce did not enjoy enough support. **MacQuarrie** also agrees with this, while **Duncan** acknowledges that Bruce had a strong claim to the throne.

THINGS TO DO AND THINK ABOUT

Try to incorporate historical opinion into your revision notes, being mindful to acknowledge points of disagreement among historians. You should link prominent historians to the main interpretations of each issue in your topic, for use in essay introductions and other areas. Meanwhile, well-known phrases from established historians, or indeed more traditional academics, may be used in Essay Questions as prompts. It would be helpful if you were able to identify the authorship while discussing that view.

 ONLINE

The People of Medieval Scotland database can be found by clicking the link on our Digital Zone (www.brightredbooks.net/subjects). It is an excellent resource for discovering information regarding all of the Scottish people known to have lived between 1093 and 1371, through contemporary documents.

 DON'T FORGET

It is essential to include historiography in each essay in order for that essay to receive more than 12 out of 25 marks. It is not necessary to refer to historians specifically by name in order to gain 13–14 marks, but relevant views on the issue in question are necessary. For higher marks, reference to specific historians is necessary.

SUMMARIES OF REVISION NOTES

FIELD OF STUDY 2 – SCOTLAND: INDEPENDENCE AND KINGSHIP, 1249–1334

REIGN OF KING JOHN, 1292–1296

The competency of King John

The portrayal of King John as an incompetent and weak king by traditional historians has been widely challenged. Many now view Balliol's failures in light of the insurmountable challenges he faced.

Both **Prestwich** and **Barrow** believe that John was no less competent than his immediate predecessors, and that his main difficulty was the absurd approach taken by Edward I. **Watson** and **Penman** believe that he was competent and was painted in a bad light by chronicles supporting Bruce. Both believe he was forced to operate under difficult circumstances. Further, **Duncan** believes that John set out to achieve a great deal, and **Nicholson** sees him as ambitious in his hopes for the Scottish crown. Meanwhile, **Young** believes that he was hampered by factionalism in the Scottish nobility and the dominance of Edward I, as does **MacQuarrie**.

On the other hand, **Beam** blames the difficulties that John experienced on the fact that he viewed himself as subservient to Edward I. **Bingham** is also critical of John's own weaknesses, citing his ability to be manipulated.

Reasons for ineffective rule

There is conjecture around why King John struggled to rule effectively. Some believe it was the result of continued factionalism among the Scottish nobles, while others blame John's inability to defy King Edward, partly due to the strength and tenacity of the English King.

C. Brown is of the opinion that factionalism was John's key issue, with many of the nobility defying him and siding with Edward. **MacQuarrie** also recognises the opposition to his reign from some of the nobility.

Meanwhile, **Oliver** sees John's difficulties stemming in part from opposition from the Bruce faction. Moreover, **Nicholson** sees weaknesses in the Scots forces amassed in 1296 as a result of the Bruces; refusal to support the Crown.

However, **Watson**, **Oliver** and **Boardman** believe that John had little chance of standing up to a king of Edward's stature. **Nicholson** sees stipulations placed on Balliol during the Great Cause and at Newcastle as undermining him from the start. Meanwhile, **Barrow** is of the opinion that legal challenges to John's authority were significant, as Edward always intended to exercise his "right". **Penman** also holds this view, although both historians make reference to King John's personal shortcomings in the face of pressure from Edward.

Alternatively, **MacQuarrie** believes the lack of training John received as a young man was significant, due to his position as the youngest of four brothers.

Meanwhile, **Nicholson** and **MacQuarrie** also believe that this shortcoming was accentuated by the breakdown in administration caused by the inter-regnum.

Blame for the invasion of 1296

Some historians believe that the Scots were themselves to blame for Edward I's invasion, while others believe that it was unjustified.

Meanwhile, **Barrow** points out that the actions of the Council of 12 and John's renunciation of homage went a long way to causing the invasion. **Young** also supports this view, stating that John was a victim of the actions of his own nobility. Conversely, **MacQuarrie** believes that Edward had planned to invade before John's defiance, after his insubordination during the MacDuff case.

On the other hand, **Oliver** believes the demands from Edward to fight for him forced the Scots into the arms of the French. Further, **Watson** is of the opinion that Edward's insistence on his Scottish overlordship and his war against France caused the Scots to turn away from England. At the same time, **Lynch** sees Edward's initial demand for military service and eventual invasion as a consequence of the crisis in both Wales and France. He also sees Edward's treatment of the King of Scotland and his demands for Scots to fight in France as inflammatory, leading to the alliance with France.

Meanwhile, **Penman** believes that John's personal weaknesses and inability to stand up to Edward were the cause of his downfall. Similarly, **Beam** claims that John gave in to Edward, and accepted his overlordship of Scotland as valid.

CONTRIBUTION OF WILLIAM WALLACE, 1297–1305

The role of William Wallace

The role of Wallace in Scottish resistance to Edward is debated. Some believe that his military successes were of note, while others are of the opinion that he achieved more politically. However, some believe that he offered little lasting impact.

Barrow believes Wallace can be seen as all the more successful as there was a lack of practical support from the nobility. He sees Wallace continuing the resistance in the name of John Balliol, as does **Lynch**, who believes that the nobility had as much to do with the early risings in 1297 as Wallace did.

contd

Summaries of Revision Notes: Field of Study 2 – Scotland: Independence and Kingship, 1249–1334

On the other hand, **Fisher** suggests that the nobility did not provide support of any significance due to Wallace's social status. **Nicholson** also sees his commitment in his continued resistance after defeat at Falkirk. **Fisher** argues that Wallace was a success, even without the support of the Comyns.

Nicholson notes the lasting political impact of Wallace after his death and suggests he was acting under his own impetus from summer 1297. Meanwhile **C. Brown** and **Lynch** note the symbolism that Wallace brought to the resistance, while **Oliver** points to the nationalistic feeling of his followers and those who came after.

The relative contribution of William Wallace to the resistance

Some historians believe Wallace was key to what was achieved between 1297 and 1298, while others suggest alternative reasons for success against the English.

Barrow has suggested that the revolt of the nobility at Irvine was key to allowing Wallace and Murray to establish and grow their rebellions. However, this opinion has recently been challenged by **Broun**, who questions the timeline of events.

On the other hand, **M. Brown** attributes the success of 1297 to a lack of competent English leadership. This is supported by **Watson**, who believes English incompetency was why Edward eventually relied upon "loyal" Scottish nobles to pursue the likes of Wallace and Moray.

Historians also champion the achievements of other prominent Scots at the time, suggesting that they were just as key to the resistance. Indeed, **Watson** suggests that arguably Moray achieved more than Wallace did before his death in late 1297, while **Nicholson** also stresses his contribution. Meanwhile, **Nicholson**, **Oliver** and **Barrow** testify to the significance of Bisset and the attempts of the nobles such as John Comyn and Robert Bruce, as well as Bishop Lamberton.

Reasons for the ultimate failure of resistance under William Wallace

Some historians support the view that other nobles may have been key to Scottish resistance, and that factionalism was key to Wallace's failure. On the other hand, some cite his lowly birth as an issue and believe that his military planning was lacking.

Watson believes that factionalism and a lack of support from the nobility hampered Wallace's attempts to resist Edward. Moreover, **Fisher** believes that Wallace's social status was an issue for many nobles.

On the other hand, **Barrow** believes that even if Wallace did not have the support of the nobility in physical presence, he had their endorsement. Moreover, **C. Brown** suggests that Wallace was not a commoner and as a result had their support.

 ONLINE

Click the link to Scotland's History section of the BBC website on our Digital Zone at www.brightredbooks.net/subjects. It provides succinct articles and videos on the Wars of Independence. Meanwhile, the Bitesize section of the website provides revision materials and knowledge tests for Higher level which would help to determine your understanding of the chronology of the topic.

 THINGS TO DO AND THINK ABOUT

In order to help you remember prominent historiography, you may want to create tables similar to the one below.

Issue	List of Factors / Sides of Argument	Supporting historians and main lines of thought
Competency of King John	John's reputation as a weak king is deserved	...
	John's reputation is undeserved	...

 DON'T FORGET

It is good practice to outline the main interpretations of a historical issue in the introductions to your essays. Use your knowledge of historiography to highlight contrasting sides of the debate before you begin detailed discussion in the main body.

SUMMARIES OF REVISION NOTES

FIELD OF STUDY 2 – SCOTLAND: INDEPENDENCE AND KINGSHIP, 1249–1334

USURPATION AND CIVIL WAR, 1306–1309

Extent of Bruce's patriotism

There is debate over how patriotic Bruce was before taking the throne in 1306. Some believe that love for his country drove him to seize the throne, coupled with support from the clergy. On the other hand, many believe he was motivated by personal gain.

Young and **Watson** believe Bruce was out for himself and determined to become king. Further, **Oliver** believes he was driven by self-interest, certainly in the time before his coronation. Additionally, **Nicholson** is of the opinion that the murder at Greyfriars was calculated.

On the other hand, both **Barrow** and **Bingham** suggest that it was not Bruce's intention to kill Comyn at Greyfriars and that he was looking to agree an approach to renewed resistance to English rule, and support for a bid for the Crown. This view is supported by **Penman**. **Nicholson** does believe Bruce was displaying patriotic tendencies, even as early as 1297, and certainly after his return in 1307 he championed the independence of Scotland. In fact, **Lynch** sees few among the Scottish nobility who put national interest before personal preservation. In the end, **Barrow** thinks that Bruce was a true patriot and acted in the interests of Scotland, even if it appeared otherwise before 1306.

Extent of support for Bruce during the Civil War

Penman believes that Bruce had less support than it seems during his early reign. This is supported by **Watson** and by **Nicholson**, who stresses the impact of the murder of Comyn in alienating at least part of the Gaelic community. Further, **Young** points to continued resistance from the Comyns after the battle of Inverurie as evidence of questionable support. Moreover, **Young** and **Penman** both suggest that sections of the nobility never came over to the Bruce side, with **Young** pointing to the 1306 murder of Comyn as the main reason.

McNamee believes that Bruce was supported by many nobles more out of fear in the early years of his reign. They opposed Bruce, as they wanted revenge for John Comyn's murder, or they feared English reprisal. Both **Penman** and **Young** point to his need of violence to subdue his enemies. However, **MacNamee** and **Penman** point to a core of support, including leading churchmen. Meanwhile, **Lynch** and **Barrow** believe that by the time of his first parliament in 1309, Bruce was secure. Similarly, **MacQuarrie** maintains that Bruce's enemies had either surrendered and were forever loyal or had been vanquished.

Reasons for Bruce's success

There is debate over why Bruce was successful in the civil war. Some believe that military achievements were key, while others promote the role of the Scottish Church, while others still point to the political environment of the time.

Nicholson points to Bruce's military know-how, and **Barrow** cites his military astuteness, especially in the way he dealt with castles. **Barrow** suggests that the myth of the Bruce was formed through his early victories and that his mercifulness in dealing with his enemies was key. **Barrow** and **Grant** both cite his use of guerrilla tactics as inspired. Further, **Penman**, **Nicholson** and **Bingham** also celebrate his skills as a military leader.

Barrow was also of the opinion that he was victorious as he appeared to be acting in the best interests of the country, while **Nicholson** points to his political acumen.

Meanwhile, **Oliver** believes that the Church had a pivotal role both in leading Bruce to seize the throne and in promoting his credentials to be king. **Barrow** is of a similar opinion, calling the support Bruce gained from Lamberton and Wishart as essential to him gaining the throne.

However, although in agreement with **Oliver**, **Penman**, points to the benefits of Bruce being free to deal with his Scottish enemies alone from 1307, due to the death of Edward I and subsequent English fragility. This is supported by **Watson** and **Nicholson**. **McNamee** supports this view, citing the weaknesses of the English after 1307, as does **M. Brown**. He believes that Bruce only appeared so militarily astute due to his enemies' weaknesses. Meanwhile, **Lynch** points to English weaknesses in Scotland, even when Edward I was still alive, as reason for Bruce's eventual success.

On the other hand, **Young** is of the opinion that Bruce's enemies were less influential at the time, due in part to the Comyns' weakened position after 1306. He suggests that Edward II was a poor leader and strategist. This is also supported by **Barrow**, who points to the weakness of the Comyns after the death of John Comyn.

Summaries of Revision Notes: Field of Study 2 – Scotland: Independence and Kingship, 1249–1334

KING ROBERT AND THE GOVERNANCE OF SCOTLAND, 1309–1320

The nature of Bruce's governance

There is discussion around the nature of Bruce's approach in controlling Scotland after the civil war.

Barrow believes there were similarities with Alexander III and that he was conservative in nature. This view is supported by **Reid**.

Meantime, **Penman** views Bruce's government in the light of an attempt to legitimise his reign, as does **Watson**.

The success of King Robert's government

There is debate around how successful Bruce's government actually was. Some believe it was a secure government which was able to exercise power throughout Scotland, with little opposition. Others claim it to have been weaker, with many opponents becoming begrudging supporters.

Both **Barrow** and **McNamee** believe Bruce's governance was very successful. Further, **M. Brown** believes that Bruce was able to gain loyalty through his approach to distributing land. This view is supported by **Lynch**, who sees the successful redistribution of land to Bruce's supporters as carried out in such a way as to transform the make-up of the Scottish nobility.

On the other hand, **Beam** believes there was, at the time, fear that Bruce's kingship was not secure and there were fears of usurpation. This view is supported by **Penman**, who points to the Soules conspiracy and Bruce's reaction to it in showing levels of opposition to Bruce. However, **Barrow** sees the threat of de Soules as minimal, while **Penman** points to inability to gain full control of the fringes of the country and of Ireland as evidence of failure.

Extent of support from the Scottish nobility

There is conjecture over how much support Bruce had from the nobility during his reign.

Barrow believes that Bruce was successful in gaining unified support, especially after 1314. **Duncan** agrees that there was no widespread opposition, while **Bingham** points to the fact that any opposition was easily dealt with.

On the other hand, **Nicholson** points to the fact that there was continued resistance to his government in the south-east of the country. **Reid** also discusses the fact that loyalty was not assumed by Bruce and was certainly not fully secure. Meanwhile, both **Penman** and **M. Brown** believe that there was an undercurrent of opposition to Bruce. Further, **McNamee** is of the opinion that there was less support for Bruce by 1320 than the Declaration of Arbroath suggests, citing a plethora of opposition detailed in English sources. **Duncan** explains much of this opposition in terms of lingering support for the Balliol succession.

THINGS TO DO AND THINK ABOUT

The following is a list of academic publications which would be useful for further research:

Geoffrey Barrow, *Feudal Britain* (Arnold, 1956)
Geoffrey Barrow, *Kingship and Unity: Scotland 1000–1306* (Arnold, 1981)
Geoffrey Barrow, *Robert Bruce* (EUP, 1998)
Caroline Bingham, *Robert the Bruce* (Constable, 1999)
Chris Brown, *William Wallace* (Tempus, 2007)
Chris Brown, *King and Outlaw: The Real Robert Bruce* (The History Press, 2018)
Michael Brown, *The Wars of Scotland, 1214–1371* (EUP, 2004)
Andrew Fisher, *William Wallace* (Birlinn, 2012)
Alexander Grant, *Independence and Nationhood: Scotland, 1306–1469* (Arnold, 1984)
Michael Lynch, *Scotland: A New History* (Pimlico, 1992)
Colm McNamee, *The Wars of the Bruces: Scotland, England and Ireland, 1306–1328* (Tuckwell, 1997)
Colm McNamee, *Robert Bruce: Our Most Valiant Prince, King and Lord* (Birlinn, 2006)
Marc Morris, *A Great and Terrible King: Edward I and the Forging of Britain* (Hutchison, 2008)
Ranald Nicholson, *Scotland: The Later Middle Ages* (Oliver & Boyd, 1974)
Alan MacQuarrie, *Medieval Scotland* (Sutton, 2004)
Michael Penman, *The Scottish Civil War: The Bruces and the Balliols and the War for Control of Scotland* (Tempus, 2002)
Maurice Powicke, *The Thirteenth Century, 1216–1307* (OUP, 2001)
Michael Prestwich, *Edward I* (YUP, 1997)
Michael Prestwich, *The Three Edwards: War and State in England, 1272–1377* (Routledge, 2003)
Fiona Watson, *Under the Hammer: Edward I and Scotland, 1286–1307* (Tuckwell, 1998)
Fiona Watson, *Traitor, Outlaw, King: Part One: The Making of Robert Bruce* (Watson, 2018)
Fiona Watson, *Scotland: From Prehistory to the Present* (Tempus, 2001)

 ONLINE

The Scottish Archive for Schools provides translations of extracts from prominent primary sources, organised thematically, and you can find a link on our Digital Zone: www.brightredbooks.net/subjects

 DON'T FORGET

To meet the minimum requirements for historiography in essays, it is acceptable to refer to relevant historians and their opinions more generally. However, to gain Historical Interpretation marks in Source-Handling questions, historiography has to be relevant and it needs to give details of a specific interpretation.

SUMMARIES OF REVISION NOTES

FIELD OF STUDY 4 – USA: "A HOUSE DIVIDED", 1850–1865

The Key Issues below are the italicised ones from which BOTH essays and source questions can be asked.

SLAVERY IN THE ANTEBELLUM PERIOD

The nature of slavery in the South

There has been debate over what constituted the relationship between slaves and their owners.

Many historians such as **Stampp** determine that cruelty and conflict was always a part of the relationship, highlighted by regular resistance. Further, **Elkins** alludes to psychological trauma and developmental issues as a result of their treatment and the culture that existed. He suggests that the relationship was very much determined by the owner, hence it was not universal. Further, **Tulloch** points to the Dred Scott case as evidence of the nature of the views of many towards slaves.

Conversely, **Phillips** takes the view that there was a level of protection given to slaves by their owners and that there was a civilising aspect to the relationship. He did not agree that it was a brutal relationship.

Fogel & Engerman also play down levels of cruelty and say that standards of living were acceptable for the time. However, this is disputed by **David** and by **Gutman & Sutch**. Meanwhile, **Penningroth** points to the ability of slaves to own property as a positive aspect.

Relative success of the Abolitionist movement

There is debate over how much of an impact the movement had.

Temperley believes that internal disagreements limited the impact they made. **Freehling** is also critical of their methods, citing the legal obstacle of state rights. Further, **Craven** believes that militancy did not help the cause, while **Litwack** believes that the views of Northerners remained relatively unaffected by their actions.

On the other hand, **Barnes & Dumond** believe that the attack on the morality of slavery by the Abolitionists was key to their increasing support. **Tulloch** also sees them as pioneers.

Reasons for ineffectiveness of the Abolitionist movement

There is conjecture over why the Abolitionists did not achieve more. Some historians believe that internal divisions were a significant factor. Conversely, others think a lack of interest in the cause was key. Meanwhile, there is also the belief that political circumstance was to blame.

Temperley believes the movement was hampered by internal disagreements regarding the methods they should use to achieve their aims. Further, **Craven** suggests that militancy hampered their progress.

Meanwhile, **Freehling** acknowledges that the division of federal and state powers exacerbated the difficulties they faced.

Litwack points out that there was not a great strength of feeling regarding race in the North.

THE PROBLEM OF TERRITORIAL EXPANSION

The issue of territorial expansion

There is discussion over why territorial expansion was so controversial and inflammatory. Some historians believe it was caused by issues surrounding slavery. Conversely, others believe tension was caused by politicians themselves and the threat of major political change.

Potter believes that the political ramifications, tied to slavery, were the main area of contention. This view is also taken by **Holden-Reid**.

Randall takes an alternative view, stating that politicians were to blame for the rising tension. This is supported by **Donald**, while **C. Beard** argues that the North saw territorial expansion as key to the expansion of business.

Meanwhile, **Holden-Reid** and **Parish** both see the political balance of power as a significant concern brought into question by expansion. Moreover, **Holt** sees expansion as having a detrimental effect on the support for both the Whig and Democrat parties.

The impact of the Kansas-Nebraska Act

McPherson is of the opinion that the Act was key to increasing militancy and was the major cause of the War. Moreover, **Farmer** suggests that it was the main reason for the growth of the Republican Party and the weakened state that the Democrats found themselves in.

Meanwhile, **Tulloch** believes the Act had significant political consequences, as it destabilised politics and threatened the balance of power in the legislature. **Holden-Reid** is in agreement, and believes that there was no longer a will for compromise between politicians of free and slave states. Further, **Farmer** points out that it began to unite the North against Slave Power.

Further, **Parish** believes that territorial expansion served to destabilise relations between free and slave states. This is supported by **Craven**, who points to the necessity for both sides to expand, especially the North, in order to grow economically.

End of the two-party system

There is debate as to what brought about the end of Democrat-Whig dominance. Some historians point to the emergence of rival parties, and incompetent politicians, while others blame issues surrounding nativism and territorial expansion, as well as social issues.

Randall believes that errors in judgement by politicians of the time led to increased sectionalism. **Craven** supports this, saying major mistakes were made by Senator Douglas. Further, **Tulloch** sees the Kansas-Nebraska Act as the immediate reason for the formation of the Republican Party. This is supported by **Farmer**, who claims the Act weakened the Democrat Party and propelled the Republicans into the limelight. Similarly, **Parish** believes the Dred Scott case also weakened the Democrat Party.

Meanwhile, **McPherson** sees pertinent issues of the time, such as attitudes towards immigration, alcohol and expansion, as key. He sees the end of the Whig Party as a direct consequence of disagreements over territorial expansion.

On the other hand, **Gienapp** believes that the emergence of the American Party began to erode traditional party support. Further, **McPherson** points to the ideology of free labour in attracting support to the Republican cause.

 ONLINE

For information on key battles of the Civil War, click the link at our Digital Zone – www.brightredbooks.net/subjects

 **DON'T FORGET**

It is essential to include historiography in each essay in order for that essay to receive more than 12 out of 25 marks.

THINGS TO DO AND THINK ABOUT

Try to incorporate historical opinion into your revision notes, being mindful to acknowledge points of disagreement among historians. You should link prominent historians to the main interpretations of each issue in your topic, for use in essay introductions and other areas.

Meanwhile, well-known phrases from established historians, or indeed more traditional academics, may be used in Essay Questions as prompts. It would be helpful if you were able to identify the authorship while discussing that view.

SUMMARIES OF REVISION NOTES

FIELD OF STUDY 4 – USA: "A HOUSE DIVIDED", 1850–1865

THE 1860 ELECTION, SECESSION AND THE OUTBREAK OF WAR

Causes of secession

There is debate over the reasons why some states decided to form the Confederacy. Some believe that it was a move to protect state rights, while others believe it was an attempt to protect the culture and economy of the South in the face of polarised Northern policy.

Grant believes that secession was a way to guarantee that the people had government that represented their wishes. Similarly, **Tulloch** believes that the emergence of the Republican Party signified possible federal opposition to slavery and hence the Southern way of life. This view is supported by **Gienapp**. Moreover, he states that the election of Lincoln caused secession. Similarly, **Holden-Reid** sees the perceived hatred of Northerners towards Southern lifestyle as key, and believes the rise of the Republican Party was evidence of that.

On the other hand, economic differences between North and South are seen as key by both **Owsley** and **C. & M. Beard**. **C. Beard** points to the impossibility of reconciling the economic needs of North and South.

Further, **Donald** believes that rising tensions were not allayed by politicians. Additionally, **Gienapp** believes that Lincoln was unaware of the seriousness of the situation in early 1861. This is supported by **Ramsdell**. Meanwhile, **Craven** takes the view that Republicans were to blame for disgruntled Southern feeling towards the Union.

Causes of the war

Some historians believe that the political system and crises in the 1850s were a major cause of the war, while others believe that the economy was more important.

Tulloch believes that Lincoln's election as president caused the War. **Craven** goes further, stating that Lincoln deliberately provoked and aimed for war. Similarly, **Gienapp** believes that Lincoln did not realise how serious the crisis was after taking office. He also believes that the formation of the Republican Party and their stance towards slavery was a major cause. However, **Holden-Reid** sees the damage having been done by Buchanan's mistakes prior to Lincoln taking up the presidency. This is supported by **Farmer**, while **McPherson** believes that Buchanan's actions around the taking and re-supplying of Fort Sumpter caused war. Meantime, **Craven** blames the Abolitionists for war.

Alternatively, **Potter** sees the political crises of the 1850s as key to bringing about war. Meanwhile, **Randall** and **Donald** see the failure of politicians on both sides to take action, in order to alleviate fears, as a cause. **Randall** refers to a "blundering generation" of politicians and the fact that war could have been avoided with more astute political leadership.

On the other hand, **Owsley** sees the social and cultural differences between North and South as key to causing the War, especially the issue of slavery. He believes that the desire to protect differing economic models led to war. **C.& M. Beard** are also in agreement that economic differences tore North and South apart.

Meanwhile **Rhodes**, **Stampp** and **Nevins** see slavery as the main driver for war. Similarly, **Holden-Reid** believes that Southerners felt they needed to secede in order to protect their way of life from the North, something that the North was not willing to abide. In support, **Potter** states that the aims of the Republican Party were so at odds with the South that war was likely. Further, **Foner** also sees the war resulting from the inability to reconcile Southern ways of life and the aims of the Republicans. He also sees the issue of territorial expansion as pertinent in the lead-up to war.

LEADERSHIP DURING THE CIVIL WAR

Assessment of Lincoln as a political leader

There is discussion over Lincoln's ability as a leader during the War.

Monaghan believes that his political leadership was sound. This is supported by **Rhodes**, who says he was vital due to his patriotism and selflessness. Further, **Randell** assesses Lincoln as an effective leader who was focused and level-headed.

contd

Summaries of Revision Notes: Field of Study 4 – USA: "A House Divided", 1850–1865

Meanwhile, **Donald** cites tension between Lincoln and Northern military leaders in the early years of the war, especially with General McClellan. However, **Tulloch** maintains that Lincoln was more visionary than they were and more aware of what was required. Further, **Williams** credits Lincoln as being an admirable military strategist. However, **Simon** questions why Lincoln did not remove some military personnel sooner.

Meanwhile, **Potter** believes that Lincoln's leadership was key to the North's victory. This is supported by **McKitrick**, who sees Lincoln's government as unified and determined.

Assessment of Davis as a political leader

There is doubt cast over Davis's ability as a leader during the War.

Potter believes that Lincoln was significantly more able and effective than Davis, so much so that it affected the outcome of the war. Meanwhile, **Gallagher** admits that he was not as competent as his Northern counterpart. Further, **McPherson** states that his personality and approach to leadership meant he was unable to get the best out of his subordinates, nor unify them to one purpose. This view is supported by **McKitrick**. Meanwhile, **Rhodes** compares Davis unfavourably to Lincoln, as does **Katcher**, who believes that he was difficult to deal with.

On the other hand, **Gallacher** believes that he was an able leader, but that his advisers and those who formed his administration were not up to the task.

Meanwhile, **Eaton** points to the fact that the South were in an unwinnable position for the majority of the War, and this was not the fault of Davis.

Assessment of Grant as a military leader

There is debate over Grant's ability as a leader during the War.

Fuller and **Harry Williams** take the view that Grant compared more favourably than Lee. Further, **Liddell Hart** believes that Grant was an effective tactician. Similarly, **Tulloch** is of the opinion that he was a modern general who recognised the reality of the war and was able to utilise the resources available to him efficiently.

On the other hand, **McPherson** is of the view that military victory was in part down to luck and circumstance outwith the control of generals on either side. Meanwhile, both **Hesseltine** and **McKitrick** cite the strength and unity of the Northern government as a key to military victory. In contrast, **Owsley** and **Donald** point to the lack of cohesion within the Confederacy as key to military defeat.

Assessment of Lee as a military leader

There is debate over Lee's ability as a leader during the War.

There is criticism of Lee as a military strategist from **Fuller**. Further, **Freeman** believes he gave too much leeway to his subordinates. **McWhinney** blames him for favouring attacking manoeuvres which wasted manpower, while **Bevin** suggests he would have been better taking a defensive approach. Moreover, **Grant** points out that it was necessary for the North to invade, while all the South had to do was defend.

On the other hand, **McPherson** credits Lee with the ability to win the war, citing circumstance as a cause of the South's defeat. Meanwhile, **Connelly** praises his integrity and credibility.

ONLINE

The National Archives and the Library of Congress both provide historic documents and sound recordings of oral histories focusing on the Civil War. Simply search on Civil War, or provide more detailed search parameters. You can find links on our Digital Zone - www.brightredbooks.net/subjects

DON'T FORGET

It is good practice to outline the main interpretations of a historical issue in the introductions of your essays. Use your knowledge of historiography to highlight contrasting sides of the debate before you begin detailed discussion in the main body.

THINGS TO DO AND THINK ABOUT

In order to help you remember prominent historiography, you may want to create tables similar to the one below.

Issue	List of Factors / Sides of Argument	Supporting historians and main lines of thought
Lee's abilities as a military leader	Lee was an able leader	...
	There were significant areas of weakness	...

SUMMARIES OF REVISION NOTES

FIELD OF STUDY 4 – USA: "A HOUSE DIVIDED", 1850–1865

THE EMANCIPATION PROCLAMATION AND ITS CONSEQUENCES

Factors leading to the Proclamation

There is conjecture surrounding the decision to issue the Emancipation Proclamation. Some historians view the decision as a result of Lincoln's own beliefs. Meanwhile, others suggest that pressure from the military and the need to look for ways to win the War were key.

Tulloch and **Stampp** are also of the opinion that Lincoln had no choice if he wanted to win the war. Meanwhile, **Holden-Reid** believes that it was a direct attack on the Confederacy and the Southern way of life. Further, it would help to weaken the economy in the South. **Fields** believes that the Proclamation was the result of Lincoln's hand being forced.

Tulloch and **Cox** also point out that Lincoln disagreed with slavery. This is supported by **Sewell** and **Parish**. Further, **Oates** and **Cox** see him as a radical looking towards major change.

Consequences of the Proclamation

Klingaman claims that the Proclamation weakened the South's ability to wage war, encouraging slave insurrection while denying international recognition to the South. **Randall & Donald** are in agreement with this.

Meanwhile, **Rawley** believes that the Proclamation increased the determination of those involved to gain victory: there was now something else to fight for. Further, **McPherson** and **Quarles** believe that the involvement of African Americans in the war greatly aided the Northern cause and pushed it towards victory.

REASONS FOR NORTHERN VICTORY AND SOUTHERN DEFEAT

Southern economic weakness

There is discussion around why the South had major economic difficulties during the War. Some believe that the problem had existed long before the war and now became more apparent. However, other historians blame mismanagement by the Confederacy and the economic strength of the North.

Thomas blames the inactivity and backwardness of the economy in the years preceding the War. This is supported by **Parish**, who believes that the South was not able to develop sufficiently in order to compete with the North.

Conversely, **Ball** blames failed Confederate policies and primarily Christoph Memminger as head of the Treasury. Conversely, **Luraghi** believes that at the beginning of the war the South was economically proactive.

However, **Ashworth** sees the financial problems suffered by the South as a direct consequence of war itself and the necessity to compete with the more resourceful North. **Holden-Reid** also cites the Emancipation Proclamation as influential.

Factors leading to Northern victory

There is debate as to what the most significant reasons were for the North's defeat of the South. Some historians point to Northern strengths, such as military leadership and political cohesion as reasons for victory. Conversely, others cite Southern

contd

weaknesses, such as a focus on states' rights and lack of international support as key.

Relative political strengths are seen as key. **Potter** points to Lincoln's leadership as a key reason why the South was defeated. Meanwhile, both **Hesseltine** and **McKitrick** cite the strength and unity of the Northern government as a key to military victory. In contrast, **Owsley** and **Donald** point to the lack of cohesion within the Confederacy as key to military defeat. They both blame this on the issue of states' rights and also on the strong opposition in the Confederate government. Moreover, **Parish** and **Crook** see the lack of international support and recognition as a reason why the South lost, although **Jenkins** points to British support for the South before the Emancipation Proclamation.

Alternatively, **Harry Williams** believes that superior military leadership won the war for the North. Further, **Fuller** believes that military leadership, particularly that of Grant and then Sherman, was key to victory. He goes on to suggest that Lee was not on their level.

Conversely, **Glatthaar** cites the significance of black soldiers to Northern victory. This is supported by **Boritt**, who cites their necessity to Northern tactics. **McPherson** and **Quarles** also believe that the involvement of African Americans in the war greatly aided the Northern cause. **Batty** and **Parish** agree that the involvement of African Americans in the war changed many Northerners' stance towards slavery. Further, **Stampp** suggests that many in the South were guilt-ridden and hence demoralised over slavery. Meanwhile, **Ramsdell** and **Merton Coulter** point to a collapse in morale.

Meanwhile, **Current** argues that economically the North was in a stronger position. This view is supported by **Foote**, who cites the industrial power of the North and its ability to overwhelm the South.

THINGS TO DO AND THINK ABOUT

The following may be found useful as core textbooks:

Alan Farmer, *America: Civil War and Westward Expansion, 1803–1890* (Hodder, 2015)
Hugh Tulloch, *The American Civil War Era* (Taylor & Francis, 2006)

The following is a list of academic publications which would be useful for further research:

Peter Batty & Peter Parish, *The Divided Union: A Concise History of the American Civil War* (The History Press, 1999)
Stanley Elkins, *Slavery: A Problem in American Institutional and Intellectual Life* (UoC, 1976)
Shelby Foote, *The Civil War, A Narrative: Fort Sumter to Perryville* (Pimlico, 1992)
Shelby Foote, *The Civil War, A Narrative: Fredericksburg to Meridian* (Pimlico, 1992)
Shelby Foote, *The Civil War, A Narrative: Red River to Appomattox* (Pimlico, 1992)
William Freehling, *The Road to Disunion: Secessionists Triumphant, 1854–1861* (OUP, 2007)
William Freehling, *The South vs The South* (OUP, 2001)
Brian Holden Reid, *Robert E. Lee: Icon for a Nation* (Orion, 2005)
Brian Holden Reid, *The Origins of the American Civil War* (Pearson, 1996)
John Keegan, *The American Civil War* (Vintage, 2010)
James McPherson, *Battle Cry of Freedom: The American Civil War* (Penguin, 1990)
Richard Newman, *Abolitionism: A Very Short Introduction* (OUP, 2018)
David Potter, *Lincoln and his Party in the Secession Crisis* (LSU, 1995)
David Potter, *The Impending Crisis: America Before the Civil War, 1848–1861* (Harper, 2011)
David Potter, *The South and the Sectional Conflict* (LSU, 1968)
David Shi & George Tindall, *America: A Narrative History* (Norton & Co., 2016)
Kenneth Stampp, *The Imperilled Union: Essays on the Background of the Civil War* (OUP, 1981)
Kenneth Stampp, *America in 1857: A Nation on the Brink* (OUP, 1992)
Hugh Tulloch, *The Debate on the American Civil War Era* (MUP, 1999)
Thomas Harry Williams, *Lincoln and His Generals* (Vintage, 2011)

 ONLINE

A link to the Abraham Lincoln Association website can be found at our Digital Zone (www.brightredbooks.net/subjects). It provides a digitised version of all correspondence and speeches made by Lincoln, with an intuitive search engine.

 **DON'T FORGET**

To meet the minimum requirements for historiography in essays, it is acceptable to refer to relevant historians and their opinions more generally. However, to gain Historical Interpretation marks in Source-Handling questions, historiography has to be relevant and it needs to give details of a specific interpretation.

SUMMARIES OF REVISION NOTES

FIELD OF STUDY 6 – GERMANY: FROM DEMOCRACY TO DICTATORSHIP, 1918–1939

The Key Issues below are the italicised ones from which BOTH essays and source questions can be asked.

GERMAN REVOLUTION AND THE CREATION OF THE WEIMAR REPUBLIC, 1918–1919

Causes of the German "Revolution"

There is debate among historians as to what was the most significant cause of the German Revolution. Some propose that defeat in the Great War was the main reason, while others believe the actions of the establishment were the cause. Others argue that popular revolutionary feeling was to blame.

Peukert is of the opinion that the roots of the revolution lay in the inability to win the war and the deteriorating conditions within the country. **Henig** is in agreement that the war exacerbated ill-feeling and tension towards the old order that already existed. Further, **Kolb** agrees with this assessment.

Meanwhile, **Carr** believes that the war cleared the old order from the political stage, making room for others, including extremists, who spontaneously rose up. Further, **McDonough** sees the psychological trauma of defeat as having profound political consequences. Both **Carr** and **Bookbinder** believe the threat from the left resulted in the declaration of a republic. Further, **Lee** believes that it was both defeat in war and the actions of the extreme left that brought about change. Similarly, **Nicholls** points to the threat from the Spartacists, as well as the mutinous actions of left-wing extremists at Kiel and Wilhelmshaven. Meanwhile, **Hiden** questions the extent of support for extreme leftist change during the revolutionary period.

The nature of the Revolution

Some historians believe that there was a revolution in 1918–1919, while others are of the opinion that only the potential for one existed.

Carr believes that politically and economically there was not much change. In support, **Hiden** sees a considerable degree of continuity. Further, **Evans** also sees the prevalence of the old order in the civil service and the army. **Peukert** and **Nicholls** also believe that the change was not a radical one.

On the other hand, **Lee** claims that movement towards a revolution can be seen, with considerable desire for radical change. Further, **Henig** points to the deep desire for significant political change and the attempt to usher in a Bolshevik-style revolution. Moreover, **Peukert** believes that at least the beginnings of a Marxist revolution can be seen in Germany. This is supported by **Henig**, who cites the fact that Ebert was able to prevent a Communist revolution.

Meanwhile, **Kershaw** and **Peukert** believe that the revolution was stalled by Ebert and the Social Democrats, who were against significant upheaval. Further, **S. Taylor** blames Ebert for allowing the old order to maintain its influence through the army, civil service and industry.

Conversely **Burleigh** and **Evans** have Ebert taking action against the radicals in order to protect the democratic institutions that had already been achieved by the revolution. In the opinion of **Weitz**, Ebert and the SPD aimed to defend democracy against the destructive power of Bolshevism. Further, **Henig**, **Kolb** and **Berger** agree that the SPD worked with the old order to ensure that democracy continued.

The nature of the constitution

Some historians view the constitution as a significant attempt to usher in a fundamentally democratic society. Others, by contrast, believe that its creation shows genuine fear for democratic institutions and that there were elements open to corruption.

Lee believes that there was an imbalance of power written into the constitution, and questions whether democracy could have developed effectively. Further, **Turner** and **Bracher** believe that the constitution compromised democratic government as a result of Article 48, while **Kolb** sees this power as revealing the true feelings of its creators towards democracy. **McDonough** agrees that Article 48 posed a real threat to democracy, but only due to the way it was employed by presidents. He believes its creators could not have been expected to predict this, in agreement with **Burleigh**. Moreover, **Hiden** sees Article 48 as a stabilising factor in the early years of the Republic.

Hiden points to the fact that it was an attempt to amalgamate different ideologies. This view is supported by **Peukert** and **Bookbinder**, who see it as an attempt to appease the majority. Further, **McDonough** points out that proportional representation does not encourage political anarchy or right-wing dictatorships and that fringe parties did not have decision-making powers. Meanwhile, **Evans & Jenkins** point out that it was significantly more democratic than what had preceded it, as does **Nicholls**.

POLITICAL AND ECONOMIC CRISES, 1919–1923

Managing threats to the Republic

There is conjecture over how effectively the governments of 1919–1923 dealt with threats to their authority. Some historians believe this was effectively managed. Conversely, others point to reliance on authoritarian means of control.

Henig notes that the Republic was not popular with the German people. Meanwhile, **Fischer** points to the fact that in countering the Communist threat in 1919, the SPD alienated the extreme left. Further, **Stibbe** is also critical of Ebert's deployment of the army, which he argues was too heavy-handed. Moreover, **Kolb** believes that the government was too reliant on the army, while **McDonough** is also critical of the fact that the government needed the army to save it, as well as of Ebert's overuse of Article 48.

On the other hand, **Lee** believes that Ebert was successful in defending the Republic against extremists. In agreement, **Carr** believes that Ebert dealt effectively with direct challenges to Weimar, although he did not eradicate the threat of paramilitary groups.

The 1923 Crisis

There is conjecture over what caused the crisis. Some historians believe the French were to blame, while others blame the actions of Germany's leaders.

Henig believes that the deliberate actions of the French in the Ruhr were the main cause. **Carr** agrees that their actions caused economic hardship.

Conversely, both **Hiden** and **Peukert** blame the economic policies of successive German governments. Similarly, **Storer** believes the government were to blame as a result of their management of reparations payments. However, while **Fergusson** agrees, he does not see the crisis as having its roots in the reaction of the German government to the Ruhr invasion.

Impact of hyper-inflation

There is discussion around how serious a threat hyper-inflation was to the Republic.

Storer believes that it destabilised the country, while **Bullock** sees it as the main threat to society in the early 1920s, encouraging the growth of extremism. Further, **Fergusson** believes that Germans now linked democracy with disorder. **A.J.P. Taylor** agrees that it did irreparable damage to the lives of the middle class. Moreover, both **Fergusson** and **Kershaw** point to the fact that hyper-inflation provided ammunition for Hitler and the Nazis.

Moreover, **Fergusson** is of the opinion that hyper-inflation had serious psychological effects on the German population. In agreement, **McDonough** argues that it was deeply traumatic, especially for the middle class. Further, **Peukert**, **Kolb** and **Bookbinder** agree that the effect of the crisis was to destroy the faith of many Germans in the new democracy.

Reasons why the Republic survived

There is debate over why the Weimar government was able to continue between 1919 and 1923 under such pressure. Some historians believe that the threats from left- and right-wing extremists were not overly serious. Others are of the opinion that the government took the necessary action, in order to avert being overthrown.

Peukert believes that neither the left nor the right provided valid alternatives to the current government. **Lee** agrees, stating that there was not united opposition in either camp. Meanwhile, **Carr** believes that the willingness of the president to use dictatorial powers saved the Republic. This is supported by **Boldt**.

On the other hand, **Lee** sees the part the army played in suppressing leftist opposition as key, while **Kolb** points out that there was no consistency in its approach to right-wing opposition.

THINGS TO DO AND THINK ABOUT

Try to incorporate historical opinion into your revision notes, being mindful to acknowledge points of disagreement among historians. You should link prominent historians to the main interpretations of each issue in your topic, for use in essay introductions and other areas.

ONLINE

German History in Documents and Images is a comprehensive site covering this topic in considerable detail. It provides a plethora of contemporary documents in translation, covering all topics that need to be studied for the exam. You can find a link on our Digital Zone – www.brightredbooks.net/subjects

DON'T FORGET

It is essential to include historiography in each essay in order for that essay to receive more than 12 out of 25 marks.

SUMMARIES OF REVISION NOTES

FIELD OF STUDY 6 – GERMANY: FROM DEMOCRACY TO DICTATORSHIP, 1918–1939

COLLAPSE OF THE WEIMAR REPUBLIC, 1929–1933

Growing Nazi support

There is debate over why the Nazis became more popular in the late 1920s and early 1930s. Some believe it was due to the appeal of Nazi policy, while others point to their organisation and effective use of propaganda. Yet others believe that there was the desire for strong leadership in the face of economic crisis.

Muhlberger suggests that the main reason was because the party appealed to varying sections of society. This is supported by **Kershaw**, who states that they were more effective at doing this than any other party, and by **Kirk**, who also highlights the high percentage of middle-class support. **Childers** also notes that party support came from varied socio-economic backgrounds. Meanwhile, **McDonough** agrees, determining that the Nazis attracted a broader section of members than any other party in Weimar Germany. He says that in terms of Nazi membership, the middle class and especially the lower middle class were over-represented. He also points to growing rural working-class support after 1930. In agreement, **Fritzsche** also points to the impact that middle-class support had on Nazi fortunes, while **Fischer** believes that the middle class were attracted by the Nazis' nationalism as well as their aura of strength and efficiency. He also sees considerable gains in working-class support in times of economic hardship and high unemployment. This echoes **Fergusson**, who sees the Nazi promise to rectify the issue of mass unemployment as reason for their growth. Conversely, **Kirk** points to a lack of support from the working class and particularly the unemployed.

Meanwhile, both **Evans** and **McDonough** point to the propaganda of the Nazi Party in portraying the party as the answer to Germany's problems. **Evans** believes that less ideologically-minded voters were attracted by Hitler's speeches and taking part in political parades. He also notes the party's popularity among the young and female voters. **Stephenson** acknowledges the impact of propaganda and emphasises that this was made possible by the effective organisation within and around the party. Similarly, **Welch** points to the positive impact of propaganda on Nazi support. Further, **McDonough** acknowledges the organisational apparatus of the Nazis which was significantly more advanced than other parties.

Alternatively, **Carr** points to the increasing number of Germans who did not trust the democratic government. In agreement, **McDonough** states that even before the Depression, almost one third of voters had abandoned mainstream political parties. **Fritzsche** and **Stackelberg** both acknowledge that the economic downturn in the early 1930s increased Nazi support.

Collapse of the Republic

Debate continues over the main reason for the collapse of the Weimar Republic. Many historians point to the economic collapse after 1929 as key. Alternatively, some point to the strength of the Nazis in the face of weak opposition. Meanwhile, others point to political intrigue in helping bring Hitler to power.

Hiden sees the collapse in terms of errors which were made in the early years of the Republic, while **McDonough** points to the refusal of the SPD and the KDP to cooperate under any circumstances. Similarly, **Stackelberg** believes that the inability of parties to work effectively together, especially the Social Democrats and Communists, resulted in the fall of the Republic. **Fischer** also points to the split between socialists and Communists as a reason.

On the other hand, **A.J.P. Taylor** believes that the Depression greatly increased the likelihood of the Nazis obtaining power. **Fergusson** agrees and has linked the growth in popularity for the Nazi Party to periods of economic strife, first in 1923, then in the period before the fall of the Republic. Moreover, **Weitz** blames the economic crises, while **Stackelberg** also highlights the Depression as a main reason. This is supported by **Bullock**. **Richards** is also of the opinion that the Depression exacerbated the already unstable political environment, while **McDonough** sees it as intensifying ill-feeling towards the republican government. Further, **Evans** believes that the Depression gave the Nazis the ability to unify the public in their favour. Meanwhile, **Hiden**, **Lee** and **Fischer** see the Depression as more of a catalyst than a cause of the collapse, leading to further Nazi support from the working class.

contd

Conversely, **Peukert** blames the way in which democratic institutions were undermined by authoritarian figures, a view that is supported by **Hiden** and by **Kolb**. Both **Overy** and **Brozart** also view the downfall of the Republic in the light of the favour shown to the extreme right in the months leading up to Hitler's appointment as Chancellor.

Meanwhile, **McDonough** believes that Hindenburg was influenced by a pernicious inner circle of advisers. Further, **Fischer**, **Fulbrook** and **Lee** also believe that the elites had to take a great deal of the responsibility for the fall of democracy, as does **Burleigh**, who believes that Papen under-estimated Hitler.

THE NATIONAL SOCIALIST CONSOLIDATION OF POWER, 1933–1934

Maintaining control

There is conjecture over how the Nazis were able to tighten their grasp on power so successfully. Some historians are of the view that the use of terror was key. Others believe that the coordination of society and their economic policies were highly effective. Meanwhile, some point to the use of propaganda.

Both **Kershaw** and **Welch** believe that propaganda was important in maintaining power, and the Hitler Myth was important as a unifying force. **Kershaw** cites its ability to stifle opposition to the Nazis and validate their actions. **Noakes** and **Gellately** are also of the opinion that the German people were encouraged by the propaganda surrounding Hitler and the national cause. Further, **Evans** believes propaganda was effective at playing on the fears of German citizens, while **Kirk** believes that it helped maintain support.

Meanwhile, **Evans** and **Wachsmann** believe that the use of terror, through the SS and Gestapo, was highly significant in maintaining the Nazis' grasp on power. In the same vein, **Kershaw** and **Geary** both believe that the violence and ruthlessness of the Night of the Long Knives acted as a deterrent to would-be challenges to Nazi authority. **Lee** believes that this strengthened Hitler's grasp on power. Meanwhile, **Stackelberg** and **Fritzsche** believe that such violence was acceptable to many Germans as a method of protecting the state. Similarly, **Noakes** suggests that the SS were key in maintaining power. However, **Gellately** believes that the security services were reliant on the general population to provide information on those who opposed the regime.

On the other hand, **Welch** points to the ability of the Nazis to use legal powers to strengthen their grasp on power. In agreement, **Benz** believes legal moves to eradicate opposition, including political parties and trade unions, was important. Meanwhile, **Lewy** points to the concordat with the Vatican as helping to limit resistance.

Similarly, **Burleigh** and **Evans** put forward the view that the Nazis used the Reichstag Fire to their advantage, helping to vanquish their enemies. Further, **Frei** and **Brendon** highlight the effects of this on securing the Nazis' grasp on power. Moreover, **Carr** and **Fritzsche** both emphasise the lucky nature of the fire for the Nazis, in that it allowed them to banish their main opposition and take a step closer to assuming dictatorial powers.

Likewise, **Evans** and **Fritzsche** point to the importance of the Enabling Act in giving Hitler dictatorial powers. Both **Stackelberg** and **Noakes** agree that this nullified the power of the Reichstag.

 ONLINE

The German Historical Institute London provides podcasts of lectures and discussions by prominent historians such as Kershaw, Fulbrook, Gregor Evans and Rodder on relevant topics. You can find a link on our Digital Zone – www.brightredbooks.net/subjects

 DON'T FORGET

It is good practice to outline the main interpretations of a historical issue in the introductions of your essays. Use your knowledge of historiography to highlight contrasting sides of the debate before you begin detailed discussion in the main body.

 THINGS TO DO AND THINK ABOUT

In order to help you remember prominent historiography, you may want to create tables similar to the one below.

Issue	List of Factors / Sides of Argument	Supporting historians and main lines of thought
Occurrence of a revolution in 1918–1919	A revolution did occur	…
	There was no revolution	…
	There was potential for a revolution	…

SUMMARIES OF REVISION NOTES

FIELD OF STUDY 6 – GERMANY: FROM DEMOCRACY TO DICTATORSHIP, 1918–1939

ATTEMPTS TO CREATE A *VOLKSGEMEINSCHAFT*, 1933-1939

Nature of the *Volksgemeinschaft*

There is discussion around why the Nazis' attempted to create a People's Community.

Burleigh and **Stephenson** agree that the Nazi dictatorship pushed anti-Semitism and race as a way of defining society. In agreement, **McDonough** says that the ability to subjugate "inferior" people on the basis of race was a key objective. **Fulbrook** also highlights racism as driving forward Nazi social policy, while **Kershaw** cites the exclusion of the Jews as a motivating factor. Meanwhile, both **Evans** and **Wachsmann** point to the belief that Germany would be re-made if race replaced class as the main organising feature of society.

Meanwhile, **Stackelberg** points to the overarching aim of national reconstruction. **Kirk** also highlights attempts to unify and gain loyalty from the young as a driving force, as well as attempts to galvanise the workforce to the nationalistic cause. Further, **Kirk**, **Pine** and **Geary** all point to the important role that women were intended to have in bringing forth subsequent generations of Germans, while **McDonough** points to the Nazis' aim of achieving unquestioning support and obedience.

Relative success of the *Volksgemeinschaft*

Some historians believe that the Nazis were able to create a People's Community, at least in part. Meanwhile others disagree, arguing that even if they appeared successful on the surface, there appear to have been failures in policy and considerable opposition to them.

Kershaw believes that the Nazis achieved their aim of removing the Jews from active society. **Evans** also points to how aggressively the Nazis pursued the creation of a racial state. Moreover, **Frevert** acknowledges that the Nazis were able to stifle the social and economic progress of females. Further, **Benz** believes that in the attempt to polarise male and female roles within society, the Nazis were successful, reducing women's presence in the workplace and higher echelons of education.

Conversely, **Stephenson** believes that there was some success, but in the end the People's Community was only partially realised. Further, **Kershaw** believes that the policy as a whole was a failure, being unable to eradicate class-consciousness, the rebelliousness of youth or ties between citizens and their religion. This is supported by **Kirk**, who believes that the People's Community existed in propaganda only, and class division remained. **Bracher** and **Stackelberg** also continue to see class division throughout the 1930s.

RESISTANCE TO THE REGIME, 1933-1939

Opposition to the Nazis

There is the popular belief that there was little opposition to the Nazis before 1939. However, a number of historians point towards significant organised and individualistic opposition.

Gellately believes that there was little opposition to the Nazis and certainly no organised resistance. Meanwhile, **Peukert** believes that there were levels of active resistance and more regular non-conformity, but that on the whole resistance had little impact, as it was unorganised. In agreement, **Kershaw** believes that opposition to the regime lacked fundamental support from the population as a whole, and hence, although regular, it came to nothing. Meanwhile, **Fulbrook** sees a German population that supported the actions of the regime in dealing with undesirables. However, she concedes that support began to break down in key sections of society in the late 1930s.

Summaries of Revision Notes: Field of Study 6 – Germany: From Democracy to Dictatorship, 1918–1939

On the other hand, **Benz** points to political resistance from the SPD and the Communist Party, who **Kershaw** says helped organise the working class. There was also religious opposition, especially from the Protestant church and Jehovah's Witnesses. Further, **Kirk** says that opposition occurred on a number of levels but was more often than not individualistic. He also notes that opposition was often directed towards individual policies rather than the regime as a whole, and hence was temporary in nature. However, both **Evans** and **Gregor** caution that individuals may have opposed the Nazis in one way but not in another, questioning if this was real opposition or what might be expected of a citizen towards their government.

Reasons for a lack of effective resistance

Some historians believe that the Nazis used terror and illegal means to dissuade possible dissenters from action. Meanwhile, some point to widespread support of the regime, partially as a result of propaganda. Others are of the opinion that opposition which did exist was poorly organised or individualistic in its nature.

Wachsmann believes that fear was the main reason why there was a lack of resistance, due to the reach of the Gestapo. He also acknowledges that those convicted of political crimes were dealt with harshly by the courts. **Kershaw** agrees that the Nazi regime brutally oppressed any opposition. **Evans** also cites the use of fear and the intimidating nature of the Gestapo in dissuading opposition, putting emphasis on its use of other agencies to help inform on opposition to the regime, rather than individual German citizens.

Conversely, **Gellately** is of the opinion that most people were conformist as a result of the benefits that they obtained from living in a police state. Meanwhile, **Evans** also acknowledges the regime's fervent use of propaganda to maintain support. Further, **Kershaw** believes that resistance was not organised effectively and hence did not gain mass support. Many in fact opposed any action against the state.

 ONLINE

Mr Marr's History site provides useful PowerPoint presentations and podcasts which summarise this topic effectively, providing details of key issues and associated historiography. You can find a link on our Digital Zone – www.brightredbooks.net/subjects

DON'T FORGET

To meet the minimum requirements for historiography in essays, it is acceptable to refer to relevant historians and their opinions more generally. However, to gain Historical Interpretation marks in Source-Handling questions, historiography has to be relevant and it needs to give details of a specific interpretation.

 THINGS TO DO AND THINK ABOUT

The following may be found useful as core textbooks:

Martin Collier & Philip Pedley, *Germany, 1919–45* (Heinemann, 2000)
Martin Collier & Philip Pedley, *Hitler and the Nazi State* (Heinemann, 2005)
John Hite & Chris Hinton, *Weimar and Nazi Germany* (John Murray, 2000)
Geoff Layton, *Democracy and Nazism: Germany, 1918–1945* (Hodder, 2015)

The following is a list of academic publications which would be useful for further research:

Paul Bookbinder, *Weimar Germany* (MUP, 1996)
Alan Bullock, *Hitler: A Study in Tyranny* (Penguin, 1962)
Michael Burleigh, *The Third Reich: A New History* (Pan, 2000)
William Carr, *A History of Germany, 1815–1945* (Arnold, 1974)
William Carr, *Hitler: A Study in Personality and Politics* (Hodder, 1986)
Richard Evans, *The Third Reich in History and Memory* (Little, Brown, 2015)
Adam Fergusson, *When Money Dies* (Old Street, 2010)
Mary Fulbrook, *History of Germany 1918–2000* (Blackwell, 2002)
Richard Grunberger, *A Social History of the Third Reich* (Weidenfeld & Nicolson, 1971)
John Hiden, *The Weimar Republic* (Pearson, 1974)
Ian Kershaw, *Hitler: 1889–1936 Hubris* (Penguin, 1998)
Ian Kershaw, *Hitler: 1936–1945 Nemesis* (Penguin, 2000)
Ian Kershaw, *The Nazi Dictatorship* (Hodder, 2000)
Hannsjoachim Koch (ed.), *Aspects of the Third Reich* (Macmillan, 1985)
Frank McDonough, *Hitler and the Rise of the Nazi Party* (Pearson, 2012)
Anthony Nicholls, *Weimar and the Rise of Hitler* (Macmillan, 1968)
Alan Taylor, *The Course of German History* (Routledge, 2001)
Alan Taylor, *The Origins of the Second World War* (Penguin, 1961)
David Welch, *Hitler: Profile of a Dictator* (Routledge, 2000)

SUMMARIES OF REVISION NOTES

FIELD OF STUDY 8 – RUSSIA: FROM TSARISM TO STALINISM, 1914–1945

The Key Issues below are the italicised ones from which BOTH essays and source questions can be asked.

THE FEBRUARY REVOLUTION

Reasons why the Tsar lost support

Some historians believe that the Tsar lost support due to the impact of World War One. Others think that popular resentment at the state of economy and social structure were the causes.

Kenez believes that there was widespread resentment from all sections of society towards Tsarist rule. Further, **Briggs** references the acute displeasure towards imperial rule, especially in the later years of the war. In agreement, **Fitzpatrick** believes that the position of the Tsar was severely compromised by the hatred of the Tsarina, regular re-shuffle of ministers and the questionable figures close to the emperor's family, such as Rasputin.

McKean believes that World War One was the catalyst that intensified the ill-feeling towards the establishment.

Reasons for the February Revolution

Some historians are of the opinion that the war was the most significant cause of the February Revolution. Meanwhile, others point to discontent with the socio-economic landscape. Some have suggested that political discontent was a driver, exacerbated by political factions and dissidents.

Wade believes that spontaneous strikes and demonstrations demanding improved conditions were the spark that ignited the revolution. Meanwhile, **Figes** notes that demand for food was also key. This view is also taken by **Corin & Fiehn**. Further, **Service** also cites social and economic conditions as important, pointing to the major shortages in early 1917.

Meanwhile, **Hasegawa** believes that the war stifled discontent that had existed before the war but then this discontent after the war effort began to falter. This is echoed by **McKean** and **Ascher**, who believe it acted as a catalyst which made levels of discontent rise to uncontrollable levels. **Volkogonov** is in agreement and thinks that the stresses of war and the incompetence of Nicholas as Supreme Commander of the army were key.

Nettl and **Service** believe that responsibility for the abdication of the Tsar lay with the Duma and the military leadership. **Pipes** and **Kenez** agree with this, saying the Tsar followed the will of politicians who convinced him to abdicate to alleviate the mutinous feeling among the armed forces. Meanwhile, **White** has suggested that Bolsheviks may have played a role in encouraging the revolution.

THE PROVISIONAL GOVERNMENT AND THE OCTOBER REVOLUTION

Growing Bolshevik support

Some historians believe that the continuing war, and its effects on the economy, was a source of discontent which garnered support for the Bolsheviks. Alternatively, others believe that the leadership of the Bolsheviks and the appeal of the party also increased support.

Figes is of the opinion that they were supported by the masses due to the popularity of their ideology. Moreover, **Fitzpatrick** suggests that the soldiers, the peasantry and the industrial workers were key. This is supported by **Smith**, who suggests that the lower classes were the driving force in bringing the revolution to its conclusion.

Meanwhile, **Service** believes that Lenin himself was able to increase support for the Bolsheviks. **Rabinowitch** echoes this, saying that the Bolsheviks led a successful campaign to gain support from the workers and lower echelons of the military.

Reasons for the downfall of the Provisional Government

Many historians believe the shortcomings of the Provisional Government were key in its downfall. Meanwhile, others believe that external events, such as the war, put untold pressures on the government. Conversely, others suggest that external opposition from new political organisations, the military and the Bolsheviks themselves were key.

Lynch notes that the unelected nature of the Provisional Government resulted in many people seeing it as wielding illegitimate power. Meantime, **Pipes** suggests that Kerensky was a weak leader, while **Service** believes that the Provisional Government lacked the ability to lead.

On the other hand, **Smith**, **Hoskings** and **Fitzpatrick** all believe that the revolution was pushed forward by the lower sections of society. This is supported by **Ponomanev**. Meanwhile, **Rabinowitch** believes that this discontent resulted from socio-economic discontent from before the war. **Figes** and **Berkman** also say that the rise of the Bolsheviks was linked to support from the people. **Service** also points to popular support for change being present. However, **Shukman** is of the opinion that the Bolsheviks had little popular support.

Howard believes that the pressures and demands of World War One, especially on the economy, were the cause. Further, **Figes** cites the June Offensive as key to the government's demise. **Acton** also believes there was great hostility from the military. Similarly, **Kowalski** also suggests that external events such as the Kornilov Revolt were to blame. **Pipes** agrees that the Kornilov Revolt destabilised the Provisional Government.

Both **Read** and **Service** are of the opinion that Lenin was key to the downfall of the government, as he appeared a stronger leader. This is supported by **Rabinowitch**, who is of the opinion that the Bolsheviks gained support from the fact that they had established themselves as an alternative to the Provisional Government.

Nature of the October Revolution

Some historians believe that a proletarian revolution occurred in October 1917, while others believe that it was a coup d'état devoid of public support.

Hoskings believes that the Bolsheviks were carried into power by the people. This is echoed by **Fitzpatrick**, and by **Kenez**, who points to the anarchic situation gripping the country. **Kenez** also believes that politically minded people were well aware of what the Bolsheviks intended.

Alternatively, **Pipes** opines that October was not a genuine revolution and in fact was a coup d'état, whereby power was seized without popular support. In support, **Figes** sees it as a small-time military coup and discounts any popular support in its execution. Meanwhile, **Williams** believes that no one really knew what the Bolsheviks stood for, so support could not be freely given. However, **Service** believes that the Bolsheviks had the support of the Petrograd Soviet and the soldiers in seizing power.

THINGS TO DO AND THINK ABOUT

Try to incorporate historical opinion into your revision notes, being mindful to acknowledge points of disagreement among historians. You should link prominent historians to the main interpretations of each issue in your topic, for use in essay introductions and other areas.

Meanwhile, well-known phrases from established historians, or indeed more traditional academics, may be used in Essay Questions as prompts. It would be helpful if you were able to identify the authorship while discussing that view.

 ONLINE

You can find a link to The Lenin Internet Archive on our Digital Zone (www.brightredbooks.net/subjects). This provides archive footage and contemporary works by Lenin.

 **DON'T FORGET**

It is essential to include historiography in each essay in order for that essay to receive more than 12 out of 25 marks.

SUMMARIES OF REVISION NOTES

FIELD OF STUDY 8 – RUSSIA: FROM TSARISM TO STALINISM, 1914–1945

THE CIVIL WAR

Reasons for Bolshevik victory in the Civil War

There is conjecture over the main reasons why the Reds were able to win the Civil War. Some believe it was due to the strengths of the Bolsheviks, including Trotsky's leadership, their propaganda and economic strength. Meanwhile, others believe it was due to weaknesses of the opposition, including in their leadership, their lack of unity and ineffectual foreign support.

Mawdsley believes that the amount of land that the Reds held was key to their victory, due to the vast economic resources at their disposal. **Pipes** also holds this opinion above all other proposed reasons for victory. He sees the Reds having superiority in manpower, industrial infrastructure and resources.

On the other hand, **Lincoln** and **Swain** point to the lack of support that the Whites had. **Mawdsley** also cites the ineffectiveness of foreign support as a reason for Red victory. Further, **Pipes** laments the half-hearted approach international powers took to opposing the Bolsheviks.

Alternatively, in contrast to **Pipes** who believes that the Whites had as much potential support for their cause as the Reds, **Figes** argues that the Reds had the support of the Russian people and were able to portray themselves as defenders of the Revolution. Meanwhile, **Service** believes that Trotsky's leadership was vital. Further, **Kenez** praises Trotsky's organisation of the army and the propaganda deployed by the Reds.

STALIN'S STRUGGLE FOR POWER

Reasons why Stalin came to power

Historians debate the factors which led to Stalin being able to assume power. Some cite the weakness of those who challenged him for power, while others cite Stalin's strengths and his luck.

contd

92

Lynch is of the opinion that Stalin was able to avoid the internal conflict within the Communist Party. Similarly, **Conquest** sees him employing unscrupulous tactics to weaken his enemies in the party, while he and **Tucker** believe Stalin was willing to compromise on ideology in order to position himself effectively. Meanwhile, **Pipes** and **Lewin** both point to his position in the Party as key to his success. Similarly, **Carr** points to his position as significant, while seeing him as pragmatic.

Further, **Lewin** believes Stalin masked his true intentions and outmanoeuvred his opponents in the party. Similarly, **Deutscher** points to the fact that Stalin was unprincipled, choosing the side that was most popular. Further, **Ward** believes that Stalin gained support from his promotion of popular ideals such as Socialism in One Country, which was avoided by Trotsky. **Cohen** supports this. **Ward** points out that many party members accepted it.

Meanwhile, **Lynch** cites Stalin's great ability as an administrator, culminating in his appointment as General Secretary of the Communist Party. Organisational control and the power of patronage were greatly significant in his rise to power. **Schapiro** points to Stalin's influence over party administration.

Alternatively, **Volkogonov** sees the ability of Stalin to rise to power as a direct consequence of the systems created by Lenin. **Lynch** also agrees that Lenin had left the Soviet Union with a tradition of authoritarian rule, and the Bolshevik system became nothing more than a continuation of the absolutist tradition seen during the rule of the Tsars.

Meanwhile, **Lynch** sees Trotsky as unable to take advantage of opportunities presented to him to undermine Stalin. **Deutscher** also blames Trotsky for underestimating Stalin and not perceiving him as a potential, or competent, rival. **Volkogonov** also points the finger at Trotsky, claiming that he was isolated in the party due to his own actions which caused disagreements with the leadership. This allowed Stalin to form alliances against Trotsky. Further, **Lewin** is critical of Lenin for not noticing Stalin's true character.

Conversely, **McCauley** believes that Stalin was lucky, citing events such as Sverdlov's death in 1919, Lenin's death in 1924, and Dzerzhinsky's death in 1926. **Lynch** also sees a degree of luck in Stalin's rise to power.

THINGS TO DO AND THINK ABOUT

In order to help you remember prominent historiography, you may want to create a table similar to the one below.

Issue	List of Factors / Sides of Argument	Supporting historians and main lines of thought
Influences leading to Bolshevik victory	Strength of the Reds	...
	Weaknesses of the Whites	...

ONLINE

The Josef Stalin Internet Archive provides publications made by Stalin, organised by theme and year. Access this by clicking the link on our Digital Zone - www.brightredbooks.net/subjects

DON'T FORGET

It is good practice to outline the main interpretations of a historical issue in the introductions of your essays. Use your knowledge of historiography to highlight contrasting sides of the debate before you begin detailed discussion in the main body.

SUMMARIES OF REVISION NOTES

FIELD OF STUDY 8 – RUSSIA: FROM TSARISM TO STALINISM, 1914–1945

POLITICAL AND SOCIAL DEVELOPMENT OF THE STALINIST STATE

Factors leading to the Purges

Some historians believe that the Purges were a result of Stalin's paranoia and fear of war. Conversely, others see social and economic motivations as key, some of which were exacerbated by the incompetence of the regime and certain individuals.

Deutscher believes that the increasing likelihood of war breaking out led Stalin to see political prisoners as a source of labour to help the economy. He and **Cohen** believe Stalin wanted to take action against those who might have challenged him. In agreement, **Conquest** sees the Purges as an attempt to secure and strengthen his own position. Both **Sakwa** and **Brendon** also blame Stalin for the Purges, while **Medvedev** sees his lust for power and fear of vengeful opponents as key factors. Further, both **Service** and **Figes** discuss the motivational fear of a fifth column and Stalin's increasing paranoia as an explanation for the Purges. **Bullock** also sees Stalin's paranoia as a driving force.

Further, **Montefiore** and **Volkogonov** blame the Purges on Stalin, but also on his inner circle. In agreement, **Nove** believes that the Purges only went as far as they did due to the enthusiasm of other officials. He states that Stalin wanted to rid the Party of unreliable members, deliberately installing Yezhov, who would go on to orchestrate the Great Purge. This is supported by **Getty & Naumov**, who state that Yezhov's appointment brought about an escalation. Meanwhile, **Corin & Fiehn** blame the NKVD for the severity of the Purges. **Gill** and **Hoskings** see the fearful atmosphere created by the security services as a driver for encouraging further denunciations. On the other hand, **Ward** thinks that the pressure put on the NKVD by Stalin was key to the action taken. **Getty** takes the view that the government as a whole was to blame, rather than just Stalin himself.

Meanwhile, **Volkogonov** believes that the Purges were Bolshevik in nature. **Lynch** agrees, saying that Lenin had left the Soviet Union with a tradition of authoritarian rule and terror. **Overy** and **Getty** also see this as a product of Bolshevism and believe that the Purges were a natural progression of violence that was the result of Lenin's leadership. **Conquest** also sees the Purges in this way: as a natural progression of the extremist policies of the Bolsheviks. He believes the ideology of such oppression came from Lenin.

Further, **Fitzpatrick** suggests that due to crises during the 1930s the Communist leadership was forced to act. This is supported by **Manning**, who believes economic failures made officials nervous about their own positions. Further, **Getty** suggests that the Purges were an over-reaction to pressure on local bureaucrats, hence evolved from below as well as above. Moreover, they were sustained from the lower ranks. **Hoskings** also sees the Purges being driven from below, in order to facilitate the advancement of Party officials.

THE GREAT PATRIOTIC WAR

Reasons for Soviet victory in the Great Patriotic War

Some historians believe that the leadership of Stalin and his generals was key to Soviet victory. Meanwhile, some see economic strength and ingenuity as key. On the other hand, others cite the mistakes and weaknesses of Germany in comparison to the Soviet Union.

contd

Summaries of Revision Notes: Field of Study 8 – Russia: From Tsarism to Stalinism, 1914–1945

Sakwa praises Stalin's foresight in tying the war effort to the idea of defending the country. On the other hand, **Mawdsley** does not think that Stalin was effective in his military leadership. **Medvedev** says that military victories had little to do with Stalin. **Nove** blames Stalin for the removal of many competent Soviet generals during the Purges. Both **McCauley** and **Service** suggest that decision-making by the Soviet generals was key to victory. Further, **Beevor** observes that their successes are all the more impressive as they were operating under a culture of fear and likely repercussions. However, **Overy** is critical of Soviet preparedness for war.

Meanwhile, **Hoskings** sees the ability of the economy to support the military as key. **Laver** also supports the work of government officials in organising the economy for war. **Mawdsley** is of a similar opinion, stating that the technical developments made in the 1930s went some way to narrowing the difference between the Soviets and the Germans.

Meanwhile, **Ward** believes that the outpouring of nationalistic feeling was key to Soviet victory. This is echoed by **Overy**, who believes that the patriotism and dedication of the Russian people, in the face of German aggression, was a reason for Soviet victory. **Kenez** is also of the opinion that the dedication of the people in resisting the Nazi regime helped win the war.

Alternatively, **Sakwa** acknowledges Hitler made mistakes, including invading too late in the year. In agreement, **McCauley** believes that the Germans were in a compromised position, having invaded and become too thinly spread. Meanwhile, **Ward** emphasises that many Russians regarded Stalin as the lesser of two evils.

THINGS TO DO AND THINK ABOUT

The following may be found useful as core textbooks:

Chris Corin & Terry Fiehn, *Russia Under Tsarism and Communism, 1881–1953* (Hodder, 2011)
Michael Lynch, *Bolshevik and Stalinist Russia* (Hodder, 2015)
Steve Phillips, *Stalinist Russia* (Heinemann, 2000)
Sally Walker & Chris Rowe, *Revolution and Dictatorship: Russia 1917–1953* (Oxford, 2016)

The following is a list of academic publications which would be useful for further research:

Anne Applebaum, *Gulag: A History* (Penguin, 2003)
Alan Bullock, *Hitler and Stalin: Parallel Lives* (Penguin, 1998)
Isaac Deutscher, *Stalin* (Penguin, 1972)
Orlando Figes, *A People's Tragedy: The Russian Revolution 1891–1924* (Random House, 2014)
Orlando Figes, *The Whisperers: Private Life in Stalin's Russia* (Penguin, 2007)
Sheila Fitzpatrick, *The Russian Revolution* (OUP, 2017)
Stephen Kotkin, *Stalin: Paradoxes of Power, 1878–1928* (Penguin, 2015)
Stephen Kotkin, *Stalin: Waiting for Hitler, 1929–1941* (Penguin, 2017)
Stephen Lovell, *The Soviet Union* (OUP, 2009)
Michael Lynch, *Stalin's Russia, 1924–53* (Hodder, 2008)
Evan Mawdsley, *The Russian Civil War* (Birlinn, 2017)
Evan Mawdsley, *The Stalin Years: The Soviet Union 1929–1953* (MUP, 2003)
Simon Sebag Montefiore, *Stalin: Court of the Red Tsar* (Orion, 2003)
J. Nettl, *The Soviet Achievement* (Thames & Hudson, 1967)
Alec Nove, *An Economic History of the USSR* (Penguin, 1972)
Robert Service, *The Last of the Tsars* (Macmillan, 2017)
Robert Service, *Lenin: A Biography* (Macmillan, 2000)
Robert Service, *Stalin: A Biography* (Macmillan, 2008)
Robert Service, *Trotsky: A Biography* (Macmillan, 2008)
Steve Smith, *The Russian Revolution* (OUP, 2002)

ONLINE

From Tsar to USSR: Russia's Chaotic Year of Revolution, an interactive article by Orlando Figes written for National Geographic, can be found by clicking a link on our Digital Zone – www.brightredbooks.net/subjects

 DON'T FORGET

To meet the minimum requirements for historiography in essays, it is acceptable to refer to relevant historians and their opinions more generally. However, to gain Historical Interpretation marks in Source-Handling questions, historiography has to be relevant and it needs to give details of a specific interpretation.

INDEX

abstract, dissertation 60
acronyms 10
acrostics 10
added value unit (AVU) see dissertation
analysis and evaluation, grading criteria 20–21

bibliography 57, 58–59, 63

contents, table of 63
course structure 4–5

description of content 6
dissertation 4–5, 42–63
   abstract 60
   basic requirements 42–43
   formatting 60–61
   keywords 44, 46
   marking criteria 60
   notes 52–55
   plagiarism 43, 56
   reading 50–51
   referencing 56–59
   research 46–47
   research questions 44–45
   structure and presentation 60–63
   unit assessment 48–49
   weighting and submission 42

essay questions 12, 14–25
   answer structure 16–19
   command words 14–15
   historic sources and interpretation criteria 22–23
   historical issues 14–15
   introduction 18–19
   isolated factor 14–17
   main conclusions 24–25
   marking criteria 16, 18–21
   mini conclusions 24–25
   wording 14–15
   writing frame 18, 20, 23
   "Evaluate the usefulness..." question 26, 28–33

fields of study 4–5, 6–7, 8
flashcards 9
flowcharts 8, 54
footnotes 56–59

grading structure 4–5

"How much/How fully...?" question 26, 34–37
information review and retrieval 10–11
"Interpretation of two sources..." question 26, 38–41
isolated factor, essay questions 14–17

key issues 6–7, 8
knowledge and understanding, grading criteria 20–21

marking criteria
   dissertation 60
   essay questions 16, 18–21
memory palace 11
memory retrieval techniques 10–11
mind maps 8–9, 54

notes
   condensing 8–9
   organising 6–7, 52–55
   research 48–49
   see also summary revision notes

optional unit assessment 4

paragraph structure 20–21
paraphrasing 27, 54, 55, 61
placement 9

question paper 4–5, 6–13
   approach 13
   timing 12–13
   see also essay questions; source handling questions
quotations 61

referencing 56–59
revision planning 7, 13
   see also notes
rhyming 11

source handling questions 13, 26–41
   answer components 26–33
   contextual development 27, 28–29, 34
   "Evaluate the usefulness..." 26, 28–33
   historical interpretations 27, 28–29, 30–31, 34
   "How much/How fully...?" 26, 34–37
   "Interpretation of two sources..." 26, 38–41
   source content provenance 26–29, 30
   source rubric provenance 26, 28–29, 30
   wider contextual development 27, 28–29, 34
   writing frame 30–31
sources 4–5, 9
storyboards 9
summary revision notes
   Germany: From Democracy to Dictatorship, 1918-1939 84–85
   Northern Britain from the Iron Age to AD 1034 64–71
   Russia: From Tsarism to Stalinism 1914-1945 90–95
   Scotland: Independence and Kingship 1249-1334 72–77
   USA:"A House Divided", 1850-1865 78–82

title page 62

writing frame
   essay questions 18, 20, 23
   source handling questions 30–31